PASTA RECIPES

Explore Pasta Pesto Sauce Cookbook Now!

(Easy and Delicious Over 100 Recipes Cuisine for Pasta)

Bruce Garza

Published by Alex Howard

© **Bruce Garza**

All Rights Reserved

Pasta Recipes: Explore Pasta Pesto Sauce Cookbook Now! (Easy and Delicious Over 100 Recipes Cuisine for Pasta)

ISBN 978-1-990169-08-3

All rights reserved. No part of this guide may be reproduced in any form without permission in writing from the publisher except in the case of brief quotations embodied in critical articles or reviews.

Legal & Disclaimer

The information contained in this book is not designed to replace or take the place of any form of medicine or professional medical advice. The information in this book has been provided for educational and entertainment purposes only.

The information contained in this book has been compiled from sources deemed reliable, and it is accurate to the best of the Author's knowledge; however, the Author cannot guarantee its accuracy and validity and cannot be held liable for any errors or omissions. Changes are periodically made to this book. You must consult your doctor or get professional medical advice before using any of the suggested remedies, techniques, or information in this book.

Table of contents

PART 1 1

INTRODUCTION 2

CHAPTER 1: PASTA AND NOODLE RECIPES 4

RECIPE 01: HOMEMADE PASTA 4
RECIPE 02: SUMMER SQUASH PASTA 5
RECIPE 03: MEXICAN PASTA 6
RECIPE 04: ANGEL-HAIR PRIMAVERA 9
RECIPE 05: SPAGHETTI WITH SPINACH AND TOMATO 10

CHAPTER 2 – SUMMER PASTA RECIPES 12

RECIPE 06: CHICKEN PASTA SALAD 12
RECIPE 07: VEGETABLE SUMMER PASTA 13
RECIPE 08: PASTA SALAD WITH EGG 15
RECIPE 09: BEEF PASTA 16
RECIPE 10: FISH PASTA 17

CHAPTER 3: PASTA SALAD RECIPES 20

RECIPE 11: PASTA SALAD WITH CHICKEN AND VEGETABLES 20
RECIPE 12: CABBAGE SOUP PASTA 21
RECIPE 13: PASTA AND SPINACH 23
RECIPE 14: PASTA SALAD WITH BACON 24
RECIPE 15: MEXICAN PASTA SALAD 26

CHAPTER 4: PASTA AND MEAT RECIPES 28

RECIPE 16: PASTA AND SAUSAGE 28
RECIPE 17: BRUSSELS SPROUTS, PASTA AND CHICKEN 30
RECIPE 18: TASTY CHICKEN BALLS WITH PASTA 31

Recipe 19: Avocado Pasta With Chicken 33
Recipe 20: BBQ Turkey Pasta 34

CHAPTER 5: PASTA DESSERT RECIPE 36

Recipe 21: Vermicelli Pudding 36
Recipe 22: Spaghetti Pudding 37
Recipe 23: Pasta Fruit Salad 38
Recipe 24: Sweet Pasta 39
Recipe 25: Fried Pasta Dessert 41

CONCLUSION 43

PART 2 46

CHAPTER 3: SEAFOOD PASTA SAUCES 47

Amazing White Clam Sauce 47
Fra Diavolo Sauce With Pasta 48
Jimmy The Saints Sausage And Pepper Sauce 50
Lobster Mornay Sauce 52
Lobster Tomato Sauce 53
Pantry Puttanesca 54
Pappardelle Puttanesca 56
Spicy Clam Sauce 58
Swedish Sour Cream And Caviar Sauce For Salmon 60
Tuna Tomato Pasta Sauce 62

CHAPTER 4: TOMATO PASTA SAUCES 64

MARINARA 64

Allpurpose Marinara Sauce 64
Basic Marinara For The Instant Pot 65
Bayys Meatless Marinara From Scratch Vegan 68

Best Marinara	69
Best Marinara Sauce Yet	70
Birdmans Marinara Sauce	71
Chunky Marinara Sauce	73
Easy Creamy Bell Pepper Marinara	75
Easy Marinara Sauce	76
Fresh Tomato Marinara Sauce	78
Hidden Veggie Marinara Sauce For Kids	79
Marinara Sauce I	81
Marinara Sauce II	82
Marinara Sauce III	84
Marinara With White Wine	85
Millers Marinara	86
Mommas Marinara Sauce	87
Rustic Marinara Sauce	88
Simple Marinara Sauce	90
Slow Cooker Spinach Marinara Sauce	91
Tomato Harvest Marinara Sauce	93
Worlds Best Marinara	95

TASTY TOMATO SAUCES 98

All Day Versatile Sauce	98
Amazing Ground Turkey Tomato Sauce	99
Amazingly Simple Tomato Sauce	101
Asparagus Mousse	102
Basic Creole Sauce	104
Basic Sauce For Pasta	106
Bayys Natural Veggie Chunky Meat Sauce	107
Best Spaghetti Sauce In The World	108

- Best Vodka Sauce 110
- Big Pot Sauce 111
- Bloody Mary Sauce 112
- Bottled Spaghetti Sauce 113
- Bryans Sweet And Hot Tomato Pasta Sauce 115
- Canning Pizza Or Spaghetti Sauce From Fresh Tomatoes 116
- Chef Johns Tomato Sauce 118
- Chunky Italian Spaghetti Sauce 120
- Courtneys Three Tomato Pasta Sauce 121
- Cucumbertomato Sauce 122
- Dads Bolognese Meat Sauce 125
- Delicious Pizza Sauce Recipe 126
- Easy Keto Homemade Tomato Sauce 128
- Easy Meat Sauce 129
- Easy Pizza Sauce Ii 130
- Easy Pizza Sauce Iii 131
- Essanayes Pizza Sauce 131
- Everything In The Fridge Pasta Sauce 133
- Field Grade Spaghetti Sauce 134
- Franks Famous Spaghetti Sauce 135
- Fresh Sauce With Artichokes And Pine Nuts 137
- Fresh Tomato Basil Sauce 138
- Fresh Tomato Sauce 139
- Homemade Italian Red Sauce 140
- Homemade Italian Sauce 142
- Homemade Pizza Sauce From Scratch 143
- Homemade Pizza Sauce Made Lighter 144
- Homemade Pizza Sauce With Olive Oil 145
- Homemade Pulled Pork Ragu In An Instant Pot 147

Homemade Tomato Basil Pasta Sauce	148
Homemade Tomato Sauce II	149
Instant Pot Tomato And Beef Sauce	150
Italian Pasta Sauce	152
Jackies Vodka Sauce	154
Marias Tomatobasil Spaghetti Sauce	156
Papa Johns Sauce	157
Pepe Vandels Spaghetti Sauce	158
Pizza Sauce I	160
Pizza Sauce II	161
Primo Spaghetti Sauce	162
Puttanesca Or Kalamata Kwik Sauce	164
Quick Enchilada Sauce	165
Quick Spaghetti Sauce	166
Roasted Garlic Bell Pepper And Tomato Blender Sauce	168
Ronnettas Spaghetti Sauce	170
Secret Spaghetti Sauce	172
Simple Delicious Pasta Sauce	174
Slow Cooker Italian Spaghetti Sauce	175
Slow Cooker Sauce With Meatballs	176
Southernstyle Meat Sauce	178
Spaghetti Sauce From The Slow Cooker	180
Spaghetti Sauce Iv	182
Spicy Creamy Tomato Sauce	183
Sugo Rosso Red Sauce	185
Tangy Horseradish Tomato Sauce For Meatballs	187

Part 1

Introduction

Pasta makes a staple in the diet of an average American, and an average American consumes almost 20 pounds pasta on an annual basis. Pasta offers energy and essential nutrients in the form of vitamins, minerals, and fiber. Pasta is healthy for the following benefits:

Cholesterol-free and Low Sodium

Pasta is cholesterol-free and low in sodium; therefore, it is healthy for everyone. One cup of pasta is a good source of essential nutrients, such as B-vitamins and iron. Whole wheat pasta offers 25 percent fiber.

Sustained Energy

Pasta supplies crucial fuel and glucose to your muscles and brain. It provides complex carbohydrates to your body that provides a slow discharge of energy. Unlike ordinary sugars, pasta sustains energy in your body instead of fleeing.

Folic Acid

Pasta is enriched with folic acid that is essential for pregnant women. Pasta contains essential vitamins, and one serving of Pasta provides 100 micrograms folic acid to your body.

- Fiber-filled vegetables and beans
- Heart-healthy fish and vegetables oils
- Antioxidant-rich tomato sauce
- Protein-packed cheese and lean meats

Whole-wheat pasta offers a considerable amount of dietary fiber to fight with chronic diseases, such as type-2 diabetes and obesity. Whole-wheat and white pasta serve as a great source of selenium and mineral that activates antioxidant enzymes for the protection of your body cells. Pasta contains manganese that is helpful to metabolize carbohydrates and regulate blood sugar. Whole-wheat pasta can increase 1.9 milligrams manganese in your body. White pasta provides a good amount of Vitamin B-9 and folate to your body. Whole-wheat pasta contains almost 113 micrograms zeaxanthin and lutein.

You can make pasta healthy with the help of lean protein, healthy fats, and vegetables. You can use olive oil and coconut oil along with chopped olives (Kalamata) and lemon juice to make pasta salad. In this book, you will learn 25 methods to cook delicious pasta. You can combine pasta with tomato sauce, meat, vegetables, pepper and even berries to enhance its taste. Follow the recipes given in this book:

Chapter 1: Pasta And Noodle Recipes

There are a few methods to prepare pasta and noodles with some particular taste and flavors. Enjoy these recipes:

Recipe 01: Homemade Pasta

Cooking Time: 15 minutes

Servings: 3

Ingredients:

- Beaten egg: 1
- All-purpose flour: 1 cup
- Water: 2 tablespoons
- Salt: ½ teaspoon

Directions:

Take a medium bowl and combine salt and flour. Make a hole in the flour and add lightly whisked egg and mix them well. You have to make a firm dough. You can add 1 – 2 tablespoons water to manage the firmness of your dough.

Sprinkle light flour on a surface and knead the dough on this surface for almost 3 – 4 minutes. Use a pasta machine or manually roll dough to get desired thickness. Use knife or machine to cut the long strips of your preferred width.

Recipe 02: Summer Squash Pasta

Cooking Time: 25 minutes

Servings: 4

Ingredients:

- kosher salt
- Spaghetti: 1/2 lb.
- Yellow zucchini: 1 lb.
- Pesto: 10 oz.
- Grated Parmesan: 1/4 cup
- Cherry tomatoes (halved): 1 cup
- Olive oil: As per need

- Black pepper (ground)

Directions:

Take a pot and fill it with water and salt. Let the water boil and cook pasta according to the instructions given on the package. Meanwhile, you have to trim the one end of zucchini and pop in the flat end into one spiralizer. Zoodles can be long, but you can cut them into 7 inches' lengths. Put noodles in one colander and sprinkle salt (1 tablespoon) on the zoodles. Mix them and keep aside.

Mix drained Zoodles in the spaghetti in the last minutes of cooking. Drain noodles and put them back in the stock pot. Mix pesto sauce in noodles and transfer to one large platter and top with tomatoes and parmesan. Sprinkle black pepper and serve.

Recipe 03: Mexican Pasta

Cooking Time: 30 minutes

Servings: 4

Ingredients:

- Spaghetti: 12 oz.
- Olive oil: 1 tablespoon
- Chicken (cubed): 1 lb.
- Onion (sliced): 1 large
- Bell peppers (sliced): 2
- Chili powder: 1 tablespoon
- Cumin: 1 tablespoon
- Dried oregano: 2 teaspoons
- Fire-roasted tomatoes: 15-oz.
- Chicken broth (low-sodium): ½ cup
- Half & half: ¾ cup
- Shredded Cheddar: ½ cup
- Pepper jack (shredded): ½ cup
- Fresh cilantro: serving time

Directions:

Take a pot of salted water and let it boil, cook spaghetti according to the instructions given on the package. Drain and set aside.

Take a large cooking pan on medium heat and heat oil. Add chicken and cook for almost 6 minutes. Sprinkle pepper and salt and mix them well. Add pepper and onion and cook for approximately 4 minutes or more to tender. Add cumin, oregano and chili powder and stir them well to coat all ingredients.

Add tomatoes to this mixture and stir this mixture well. Add half-and-half and chicken broth and stir. Add spaghetti (cooked) to your cooking pan and toss to coat all ingredients. Add cheese and cream in this mixture and garnish with chopped cilantro. Serve hot.

Recipe 04: Angel-Hair Primavera

Cooking Time: 45 minutes

Servings: 4

Ingredients:

- Angel hair: 12 oz.
- Broccoli florets: 2 cups
- kosher salt
- Cherry tomatoes (red and yellow): 1 pt.
- Baby-bella mushrooms: 1 8-oz.
- Artichoke hearts (drained & chopped): 15-oz.
- Garlic powder: 2 teaspoons
- Black pepper: ground
- Grated Parmesan: 3/4 cup + for garnishing
- Chopped basil

Directions:

Preheat an oven to almost 400 degrees F. Take a large pot with salt and water, let it boil and cook pasta as per instructions that are given on the package. Drain and reserve one cup pasta water. Return this water to the pot and keep it aside.

Take a baking sheet and add a mixture of artichoke hearts, tomatoes, toss broccoli, olive oil, garlic powder, mushrooms, pepper, and salt. Roast it for almost 15 to 20 minutes.

Add vegetables to the pot with pasta water and cook on low heat. Mix well to create a thick sauce. You can add extra pasta water as per your needs.

Garnish with basil and parmesan and serve hot.

Recipe 05: Spaghetti With Spinach And Tomato

Cooking Time: 20 to 30 minutes

Servings: 4

Ingredients:

- Spaghetti: 12 oz.
- Olive oil: 1 tablespoon
- Chopped Garlic: 2 cloves
- Italian sausage (cooked) links (sliced): 3/4 lb.
- Baby Spinach: 3 cups

- Sun-dried tomatoes (chopped): ½ cup
- Chicken broth (low-sodium): ¾ cup
- Heavy cream: ¾ cup
- kosher salt
- Black pepper as per taste
- Grated Parmesan: Garnishing

Directions:

Take one large pot with salt and water. Let this water boil and cook spaghetti as per instructions given on the package.

Take a large pot and put it on medium heat. Now, heat oil and cook garlic to get fragrance for one minute. Add spinach, dried tomatoes and sausage and cook them until sausage turns brown and spinach is completely cooked. It will take almost 3 – 5 minutes. Add heavy cream and chicken broth to let them simmer. Let the sauce turn creamy and add spaghetti to this pan. Toss spaghetti with sauce and sprinkle pepper and salt. Garnish with cilantro and parmesan and serve hot.

Chapter 2 – Summer Pasta Recipes

If you want something delicious and healthy in the summer season, there are a few recipes for you:

Recipe 06: Chicken Pasta Salad

Cooking Time: 1 hour

Servings: 3 to 4

Ingredients:
- 6oz whole wheat pasta
- 2 tomatoes, chopped
- 1 yellow bell sliced pepper
- 1 cup chopped cauliflower
- Cooked Chicken (cubed): 1 cup
- 1 3-4oz sliced olives
- 1 small chopped yellow onion
- 1/2 cup butter
- 1 tablespoon sugar

- 2 tablespoons vinegar
- Salt & pepper as per taste

Instructions:

In the first step, take salted boiling water and cook pasta as per the instructions given on the packet. It will be good to add cauliflower in water before removing pasta from heat. Let it cook for almost 45 minutes and throw the water and rinse the Pasta and cauliflower with cold water.

In a large bowl, add pasta, onions, bell pepper, cauliflower, chicken and tomato. Mix them well and then add black olives, sugar, vinegar, salt, and pepper. Mix all the ingredients well and keep in a refrigerator before serving time.

Recipe 07: Vegetable Summer Pasta

Cooking Time: 1 hour
Servings: 04
Ingredients:

- 6oz pasta
- 2 medium tomatoes, chopped
- 1 small chopped onion
- Chopped cabbage: 1 cup
- 4oz sliced olives
- 1/4 cup fat-free mayonnaise
- 1 tablespoon brown sugar
- 2 tablespoons vinegar
- Salt & pepper as per taste

Directions:

In the first step, cook pasta as per the instructions that are given on the packet. It will be good to add cabbage in water before removing the pasta from heat. Let it cook for 45 minutes and then throw the water and rinse the Pasta and Broccoli with cold water.

In a large bowl, add pasta, onions, cabbage, and tomato. Mix them well and then add black olives, sugar, vinegar, salt, and pepper. Mix all the ingredients well and keep in a refrigerator before serving them.

Recipe 08: Pasta Salad With Egg

Cooking Time: 25 minutes

Servings: 4

Ingredients:

- Eggs: 8
- Paprika: 1 teaspoon
- Bacon (chopped strips): ½ cup
- Minced Red onion: ½
- Mayonnaise: 1 tablespoon
- Pasta: 7 oz
- Pepper and salt
- Dijon Mustard: 2 tablespoons
- Dill weed: 1 tablespoon

Directions:

Boil eggs and peel them to chop into small pieces. Keep them aside.

Cook pasta as per instructions given on the package and keep it aside.

Take a large bowl and mix mustard, mayonnaise, egg, dill, onion, salt, pepper, bacon, pasta and paprika. Mash all these ingredients well with a wooden spoon or fork. Serve with your favorite sauce.

Recipe 09: Beef Pasta

Cooking Time: 1 hour

Servings: 3 to 4

Ingredients:

- 6oz whole wheat pasta
- 2 tomatoes, chopped
- 1 yellow bell sliced pepper
- 1 cup chopped cauliflower
- Cooked beef (cubed): 1 cup
- 1 3-4oz sliced olives
- 1 small chopped yellow onion

- 1/2 cup butter
- 1 tablespoon sugar
- 2 tablespoons vinegar
- Salt & pepper as per taste

Instructions:

In the first step, take salted boiling water and cook pasta as per the instructions given on the packet. It will be good to add cauliflower in water before removing pasta from heat. Let it cook for almost 45 minutes and throw the water and rinse the Pasta and cauliflower with cold water.

In a large bowl, add pasta, onions, bell pepper, cauliflower, beef and tomato. Mix them well and then add black olives, sugar, vinegar, salt, and pepper. Mix all the ingredients well and keep in a refrigerator before serving time.

Recipe 10: Fish Pasta

Cooking Time: 30 minutes

Servings: 4

Ingredients:

- Spaghetti: 12 oz.
- Olive oil: 1 tablespoon
- Cooked Fish (cubed): 1 lb.
- Onion (sliced): 1 large
- Cauliflower: 2
- Chili powder: 1 tablespoon
- Cumin: 1 tablespoon
- Dried oregano: 2 teaspoons
- Fire-roasted tomatoes: 15-oz.
- Chicken broth (low-sodium): ½ cup
- Half & half: ¾ cup
- Shredded Cheddar: ½ cup
- Pepper jack (shredded): ½ cup
- Fresh cilantro: serving time

Directions:

Take a pot of salted water and let it boil, cook spaghetti according to the instructions given on the package. Drain and set aside.

Take a large cooking pan on medium heat and heat oil. Add fish and cook for almost 6 minutes. Sprinkle pepper and salt and mix them well. Add pepper and onion and cook for approximately 4 minutes or more to tender. Add cumin, oregano and chili powder and stir them well to coat all ingredients.

Add tomatoes to this mixture and stir this mixture well. Add half-and-half and chicken broth and stir. Add spaghetti (cooked) to your cooking pan and toss to coat all ingredients. Add cheese and cream in this mixture and garnish with chopped cilantro. Serve hot.

Chapter 3: Pasta Salad Recipes

If you want pasta salad, you can get the advantage of these recipes. There are a few essential recipes for your help:

Recipe 11: Pasta Salad With Chicken And Vegetables

If you want something delicious and healthy in the summer season, there are a few recipes for you:

Total Cooking Time: 15 to 30 minutes

Servings: 2 to 3

Ingredients:
- 4-ounce cooked chicken meat
- 2 chopped tomatoes
- Cabbage: 1 cup
- 10-ounce romaine salad

- 1/4 cup fresh cheese
- Pasta: 6 oz.

Directions:

Cook pasta according to the instructions given on the package.

Grill chicken on a griller on medium heat. Grill chicken meat for almost 2 to 3 minutes and turn its sides to let it done properly. Now remove from grill, let it cool and make cubes.

Now, gently mix cabbage, chicken cubes tomato and lettuce in a large bowl. Mix pasta and equally divide salad among four bowls and sprinkle 1 tablespoon of cheese on every serving.

Recipe 12: Cabbage Soup Pasta

Cooking Time: 40 minutes
Servings: 6
Ingredients:
- 3 cloves garlic

- 1 onion
- 8oz. pasta
- 2 to 3 carrots
- 1.5 cups cabbage
- 1.5 cups cut beans
- Handful spinach
- Salt to taste
- 1.5 cups peas
- 8 cups vegetable broth
- 1.5 cups corn
- 15 oz. diced tomatoes
- Rice and herbs

Directions:

Cook pasta as per instructions given on the package and keep aside.

Chop all vegetables and cook in the stockpot on the medium heat. Cook for 5 to 7 minutes and add garlic to cook for 30 seconds. Now add the broth and cook all vegetables except spinach. Reduce heat and cook for 20 to 30 minutes to make the vegetables soft. Add pasta and mix these ingredients well. Now mix the spinach and salt as per taste. Serve hot.

Recipe 13: Pasta And Spinach

Cooking Time: 30 minutes

Servings: 4

Ingredients

- 1-pound grilled chicken, trimmed
- 3 nectarines, halved
- 1/4 cup balsamic vinaigrette, light
- 6-ounce baby spinach, fresh
- Pasta: 8oz.
- 1/4 cup feta cheese
- Black Pepper, ground (Optional)

Directions:

Prepare a grill.

Cut chicken to make small strips with a sharp knife and grill on a grill rack greased with cooking spray. You can grill each side for five minutes at 160° (check thermometer). It is time to grill nectarines for 4 to 5 minutes on every side and remove both chicken and nectarine from the grill. Leave it for 10 minutes.

Cook pasta as per instructions given on the package and keep it aside.

Use a sharp knife to divide nectarine into slices and make thin slices of chicken. Mix vinaigrette and spinach in a large bowl. Add pasta and mix it gently to coat everything. It is time to divide spinach mixture equally in 6 plates. Now top every plate equally with nectarine and chicken slices. Sprinkle cheese and pepper as per your taste.

Recipe 14: Pasta Salad With Bacon

Cooking Time: 30 to 45 Minutes

Serving: 4

Ingredients:

- 1/4 teaspoon black pepper, ground
- Pasta: 8 ounces
- 1/4 teaspoon salt

- 1/4 cup fresh onion, minced
- 6-ounce chicken breast without skin
- 2 bacon, slices
- 3/4 cup apple cider, without sugar
- 1/2 cups chicken broth, without salt and fat

Directions:

Cook pasta as per instructions given on the package.

Take a chicken breast and keep between 2 durable plastic sheets to make a wrap. The meat should be ½ inch thick and you can use a rolling pin to make it flat. Sprinkle salt and pepper on chicken.

Now, take a large cooking pan to cook bacon on medium heat to make it crisp. Remove this bacon from a cooking pan and add chicken in the similar pan. Cook every side for six minutes or until it is completely done. Remove this chicken from the pan and keep it warm.

Now add onion in the cooking pan and cook for two minutes, stir the spoon frequently and add broth and cider. Let it boil and scrape the pan to drop brown bits in the soup. Cook the both mixtures to reduce the broth to ½ cup. It may take five minutes. It is time to mix cooked bacon and pasta and serve with sauce on chicken.

Recipe 15: Mexican Pasta Salad

Cooking Time: 30 minutes

Servings: 4

Ingredients:

- Spaghetti: 12 oz.
- Olive oil: 1 tablespoon
- Beef (cubed): 1 lb.
- Onion (sliced): 1 large
- Chili powder: 1 tablespoon
- Cumin: 1 tablespoon
- Dried oregano: 2 teaspoons
- Tomato Paste: 15-oz.
- Beef broth (low-sodium): ½ cup
- Half & half: ¾ cup
- Shredded Cheese: ½ cup
- Pepper jack (shredded): ½ cup
- Fresh cilantro: serving time

Directions:

Take a pot of salted water and let it boil, cook spaghetti according to the instructions given on the package. Drain and set aside.

Take a large cooking pan on medium heat and heat oil. Add beef and cook for almost 6 minutes. Sprinkle pepper and salt and mix them well. Add onion and cook for approximately 4 minutes or more to tender. Add cumin, oregano and chili powder and stir them well to coat all ingredients.

Add tomatoes paste to this mixture and stir this mixture well. Add half-and-half and broth and stir. Add spaghetti (cooked) to your cooking pan and toss to coat all ingredients. Add cheese and cream in this mixture and garnish with chopped cilantro. Serve hot.

Chapter 4: Pasta And Meat Recipes

You can try these meat and pasta recipes to improve your health. These are really delicious for everyone!

Recipe 16: Pasta And Sausage

Cooking Time: 30 minutes
Servings: 4
Ingredients:
- 3 tablespoons olive oil
- 8 eggs
- 12 oz crumbled Italian sausage
- ½ chopped onion
- 1 cup cheese (ricotta)
- 2 cups chopped spinach
- ½ teaspoon sea salt
- Pasta: 8 ounce

- 1 cup chopped mushrooms
- ¼ cup chopped cheese (Parmesan)

Directions:

Cook pasta as per instructions given on the package.

Prepare an oven at 350º F. Whisk eggs in a medium bowl and mix olive oil in the mixture. Keep it aside.

Take an oven proof pan and cook onion and sausage in a medium heat with one tablespoon olive oil. Let the onions turn light brown and then add pepper and salt. Now add spinach and cover it after mixing it. After 2 minutes, add ricotta, salt, and mushrooms. It is time to pour the eggs and pasta, and mix this blend well. Now cover it on a medium heat for 3 minutes.

Now sprinkle parmesan cheese on the top and keep this pan in over for almost 20 minutes. After removing from oven, let it cool for five minutes and then release it from the edges with a spatula. Divide it into slices before serving.

Recipe 17: Brussels Sprouts, Pasta And Chicken

Cooking Time: 30 minutes

Servings: 4

Ingredients:
- 2 cloves crushed garlic
- 2 tablespoons coconut oil
- 1 chopped onion
- 1 pound Brussels sprouts, bisected
- 1 sweet potato, cubed
- ¼ cup Parmesan cheese (grated)
- Cooked Pasta: 8 oz.
- 4 ounces chopped mushrooms
- 12 oz ham, (precooked and cubed)
- 1 teaspoon sea salt

- 4 eggs

Directions:

Cook pasta as per instructions given on the package.

Prepare an oven in advance at 350ºF.

Take a large skillet and cook garlic and onion with oil on a medium heat for 2 minutes. Now add Brussels, potato, mushrooms and salt. Mix it well and then cover for 7 to 8 minutes. You can mix it occasionally. Now mix ham and pasta, and use 4 spoons to make depressions in the mixture. Now crack an egg into each depression and sprinkle cheese on the top.

Transfer the pan in oven and bake for 10 minutes.

Recipe 18: Tasty Chicken Balls With Pasta

Cooking Time: 1 hour 10 minutes

Servings: 5

Ingredients:

- ¾ cup hot sauce
- ½ cup butter, melted

- 1 teaspoon sea salt
- 2 tablespoons vinegar
- 1 cup sour cream
- Blue Cheese (Dressing)
- 1 cup mayonnaise
- Pasta: 8 oz.
- ½ teaspoon sea salt
- 3 pounds chicken mince
- 1 cup crushed cheese
- Carrot sticks

Directions:

Cook pasta as per instructions given on your package.

To make the balls, take a small bowl and prepare a mixture of vinegar, butter, sauce, and salt. Now mix it well. Separate ¼ cup of this mixture and set it aside. Add chicken mince and make small balls with this mixture. Now take the marinade in a large bowl and add chicken balls in this mixture. Mix the balls and keep in the refrigerator for 60 minutes.

Dressing:

Take a small bowl mix cheese, mayonnaise, salt, and sour cream. Mix it well and keep in refrigerator until you serve it.

Now keep an oven rack in the broiler with 8" height. Now preheat a broiler and cover the baking sheet with foil. Keep the balls in a row on the baking sheet with consistent space. Let it broil for 14 to 16 minutes and turn once. Keep this procedure continue until you make the balls crispy. Keep an eye on the balls to avoid burning.

Now transfer pasta on the serving plate, put meatballs on pasta and spread the hot sauce mixture on the top and serve with dressing and carrot sticks.

Recipe 19: Avocado Pasta With Chicken

Cooking Time: 10 minutes
Servings: 6
Ingredients:
- 1 chopped poblano pepper
- Pasta: 8 oz.
- 1 chopped tomato
    - 1 lime
- ¼ teaspoon sea salt
- ½ chopped onion

- Chicken (cooked and cubed): 2 cups
- 3 tablespoons chopped cilantro
- ¼ teaspoon cayenne pepper
- 4 avocados, halved (pitted)

Directions:

Cook pasta as per instructions given on the package.

Take a medium bowl and mix pepper, tomato, onion, cilantro, chicken and salt. Take one spoon of the mixture and keep it in the avocado half. You can scoop out some pulp to use in the salsa. Spread pasta in a plate and top it with avocado. Sprinkle lime juice on it and serve. You can use tuna in salsa as well.

Recipe 20: Bbq Turkey Pasta

Cooking Time: 30 minutes

Servings: 4

Ingredients:

- 1 pound raw turkey breast

- ½ teaspoon cayenne pepper
- ½ chopped bell pepper
- ½ chopped onion
- Pasta: 8 oz.
- ½ chopped red pepper
- 1 cup barbecue sauce
- 4-grain hamburger rolls, sliced

Directions:

Cook pasta as per instructions given on the package.

Great a nonstick cooking pan with cooking oil and add the turkey to let it brown. It may take almost 10 minutes. Remove any liquid and add onion and peppers to cook almost 3 minutes. Add cayenne pepper and barbecue sauces and cook for almost 2 minutes. Take one-half of the half and top with turkey mixture and cover with another half of the bun. Serve with pasta and a low fat and low sugar sauce.

Chapter 5: Pasta Dessert Recipe

If you want to enjoy sweet desserts, there are a few recipes for you. These are extremely delicious and healthy:

Recipe 21: Vermicelli Pudding

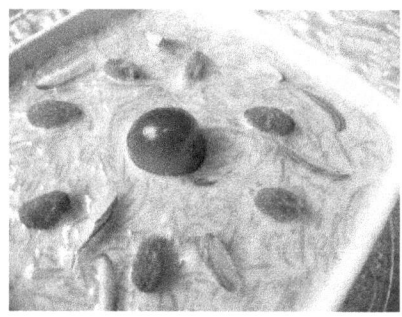

Cooking Time: 40 minutes

Servings: 4

Ingredients:

- Milk: 1-quart
- White sugar: 5 tablespoons
- Vermicelli pasta (broken): 8 ounce
- Raisins: 8
- Cardamom seeds: 8

Directions:

Pour milk in one saucepan and add cardamom seeds and sugar. Let them boil on medium heat and reduce heat to simmer for almost 5 minutes. Mix raisins and broken pasta into milk and let them cook for almost 5 minutes to let the cream thick. Turn off heat and leave this mixture for almost 15 minutes. If the pudding is thick, you can add little milk. Serve hot.

Recipe 22: Spaghetti Pudding

Cooking Time: 55 minutes

Servings: 4

Ingredients:

- Butter: 2 tablespoons
- Milk: 2 cups
- Chopped cashews: 2 tablespoons
- Uncooked pasta: 4 ounces
- White sugar: 6 tablespoons
- Raisins: 2 tablespoons

Directions:

Take a large cooking pan and put it on medium heat to melt butter. Fry raisins and cashews to turn them golden brown. Remove these ingredients from pan and keep it aside. Fry pasta (dry) pieces in the pan to let them golden brown for almost 5 minutes.

Add milk to this pan and increase heat. Let the milk boil and reduce heat to low. Simmer until the spaghetti turns soft and the milk turns thick. Mix cashews, raisins and sugar. Take off from heat and leave for 30 minutes. Serve cold or hot.

Recipe 23: Pasta Fruit Salad

Cooking Time: 1 hours 15 minutes

Servings: 7

Ingredients:
- Macaroni: 12 ounces
- Vanilla pudding mix: 3.5 ounce
- Milk: 1 ½ cups
- Mandarin oranges (drained): 11 ounces
- Crushed pineapple: 20 ounce
- Fruit cocktail (drained): 15.25 ounce

- Maraschino cherries (drained): 10 ounces
- Whipped topping: 8 ounces

Directions:

Take salted water in a pot and let it boil. Cook pasta according to the instructions given on the package and rinse under water.

Follow the directions of pudding to prepare it, but use only 1.5 cups milk and keep in refrigerator to chill.

Take a large bowl and mix pudding and pasta. Mix these ingredients well and add fruit cocktail, pineapples, oranges and cherries. Mix whipped cream and serve chilled.

Recipe 24: Sweet Pasta

Cooking Time: 15 minutes

Servings: 8

Ingredients:

- Half-and-half: 1 pint

- Lemon zest: 1 lemon
- Orange zest: 1 orange
- Honey: 2 tablespoons
- Kosher salt: 1 pinch
- Linguine: 12 ounces
- Lemon juice: 1 tablespoon
- Semisweet chocolate: 3 ounces
- Hazelnuts (chopped): 1/4 cup

Directions:

Take one large pot filled with salted water and boil water on high heat.

Take a heavy skillet and pour cream to heat it. Add salt, zest and honey to cook on medium heat. Be careful because the cream shouldn't boil so mix occasionally for almost 4 minutes.

In the meantime, add pasta to boiling water and cook until tender. Mix occasionally for almost 2 to 3 minutes. Drain pasta and put it in the heavy skillet with cream. Add lemon juice and mix well.

Take serving dishes and transfer pasta to dishes. Garnish with chocolate and hazelnuts. Serve.

Recipe 25: Fried Pasta Dessert

Cooking Time: 30 minutes

Servings: 2 to 3

Cooking Time: 30 minutes

Servings: 2 to 3

Ingredients:

- Angel-hair pasta: 1/3 pound
- Vanilla beans: 2
- Crème Fraiche: 1 cup
- Honey divided: 4 tablespoons
- Orange zest: 1 teaspoon
- Lemon zest: 1 teaspoon
- One pinches cinnamon
- Vegetable oil, for frying
- Toasted walnuts: 2 tablespoons

Directions:

Cook pasta as per instructions that are given on the package, drain and keep it aside.

Take a bowl, whisk vanilla seeds, cream and honey (1 tablespoon). Mix them well and set aside.

Take another bowl and whisk remaining honey, lemon zest, and orange zest along with cinnamon. Keep this bowl aside.

Take a deep pan, heat oil on high flame and once the temperature reaches 375 degrees F, fry cooked pasta in twirled haystacks. Flip every haystack halfway until it becomes golden and crispy. In the absence of a thermometer, you can put one pinch cornstarch to your pan because it will fry immediately as your oil is ready to cook pasta.

Set pasta on a plate, drizzle honey mixture and cream sauce. Garnish with walnuts and serve.

Conclusion

recipes of the pasta diet because the unique combination of ingredients will keep you full and reduce your craving. The fresh fruits and vegetables are high in fiber and more filling. You can't consume starchy vegetables because they are greater in calories. Pasta has specific options of power foods, such as considering ten types of canned soups and select one with less salt and sugar. You need more fiber and healthy fat in your regular diet. They offer hundreds of recipes with their particular points that you can eat during your diet. If your prepared dish is not available in their provided database, then you can calculate calories of a particular dish on a free tool.

Include Proteins in Your Regular Diet

Protein should be an important part of your diet to get rid of stubborn belly fat. You can follow a diet for almost two months with 30% protein, 40% carbs, and 30% healthy fat. It will prove helpful to get rid of additional belly fat. Including protein in your diet will be a long term strategy for you to lose weight.

Avoid Sugar and Sugar Beverages

You need to avoid liquid sugar because it is worse for you as your brain can't acknowledge the liquid sugar in the same way as solid calories. If you drink the more sugar-sweetened drink, then you will end up eating more calories.

Cut Carbohydrates from Your Diet

If you want to reduce belly fat, then you should cut carbohydrates from your regular diet. By decreasing carbs, your hunger will go down, and you may lose weight. You need to follow a low-carb and low-fat diet to target your belly fat. Avoid white bread, rice, and pasta and keep your protein intake high. If you want to lose weight fast, then it is important to cut down your carb intake up to 50 grams per day.

Eat Fiber Rich Food

Try to include green leafy vegetables and fresh fruits in your regular diet. It will help you to get rid of belly fat. Fresh fruits and vegetables will prove helpful, and you should take almost 14 grams of fiber on a regular basis for a 10% decrease in the calorie intake. It helps you have a flat belly and reduce harmful belly fat.

Make a Food Journal

It is important to keep a record of how much you are eating because excessive consumption of fiber and protein will be harmful to you. If you want to boost the 25 to 30% protein intake, then you have to write it in a food journal to calculate the total calories you need to consume in a day.

Do's and Don'ts of Healthy Diet

- You can load your regular meals with fruits and vegetable-carrying low calories because these are higher in fiber and can easily satisfy your craving.

- Stick to your calorie target because these are assigned to you by protein, carb, calories, fiber and fat requirements of your body. It is also based on the fact that how hard your body can do the workout to burn off the fat. You can check calories with your smartphone or web.

- Alcohol is not good to overdo them. Use it in moderation because 12-ounce beers often low-calories. If you spend all the points in the alcohol intake, then what will you do for the rest of the day.

Part 2

Chapter 3: Seafood Pasta Sauces

Amazing White Clam Sauce

"I got this recipe from an old boyfriend, and have modified it over the years. My husband and I have this at least every two weeks with a big loaf of garlic bread. It's very easy, but very delicious and filling."

Serving: 4 | Prep: 5 m | Cook: 1 h | Ready in: 1 h 5 m

Ingredients
- 1/2 cup olive oil
- 1 large onion, chopped
- 6 cloves garlic, minced
- 1 pinch red pepper flakes, or to taste
- 1 3/4 cups half-and-half cream
- 3 (6.5 ounce) cans minced clams, drained with juice reserved
- 1/4 cup grated Parmesan cheese for topping
- 1 (8 ounce) package dried linguine pasta

Direction

- Heat olive oil in a large skillet over medium-high heat. Add onion and red pepper flakes, and cook stirring constantly until onion is tender. Add garlic, and cook for a couple of minutes, just until fragrant. Pour in the reserved clam juice, and simmer over low heat for 10 minutes.
- Gradually stir the half-and-half cream into the skillet, and simmer for another 20 minutes, but do

not boil. At this time, I like to prepare my linguine and garlic bread.
- Bring a large pot of lightly salted water to a boil. Add linguine pasta, and cook for 8 to 10 minutes, until al dente.
- Add clams to the sauce, and cook just until clams are heated through, or they will become tough and chewy. Remove from heat, and serve over linguine pasta. Top with a sprinkle of grated Parmesan cheese.

Nutrition Information

- Calories: 825 calories
- Total Fat: 44.7 g
- Cholesterol: 136 mg
- Sodium: 280 mg
- Total Carbohydrate: 57.5 g
- Protein: 48.6 g

Fra Diavolo Sauce With Pasta

"This sauce includes shrimp and scallops, best served with linguine pasta."

Serving: 8 | Prep: 20 m | Cook: 40 m | Ready in: 1 h

Ingredients
- 4 tablespoons olive oil, divided
- 6 cloves garlic, crushed
- 3 cups whole peeled tomatoes with liquid, chopped
- 1 1/2 teaspoons salt
- 1 teaspoon crushed red pepper flakes

- 1 (16 ounce) package linguine pasta
- 8 ounces small shrimp, peeled and deveined
- 8 ounces bay scallops
- 1 tablespoon chopped fresh parsley

Direction

- In a large saucepan, heat 2 tablespoons of the olive oil with the garlic over medium heat. When the garlic starts to sizzle, pour in the tomatoes. Season with salt and red pepper. Bring to a boil. Lower the heat, and simmer for 30 minutes, stirring occasionally.
- Meanwhile, bring a large pot of lightly salted water to a boil. Cook pasta for 8 to 10 minutes, or until al dente; drain.
- In a large skillet, heat the remaining 2 tablespoons of olive oil over high heat. Add the shrimp and scallops. Cook for about 2 minutes, stirring frequently, or until the shrimp turn pink. Add shrimp and scallops to the tomato mixture, and stir in the parsley. Cook for 3 to 4 minutes, or until the sauce just begins to bubble. Serve sauce over pasta.

Nutrition Information

- Calories: 335 calories
- Total Fat: 8.9 g
- Cholesterol: 52 mg
- Sodium: 655 mg
- Total Carbohydrate: 46.3 g
- Protein: 18.7 g

Jimmy The Saints Sausage And Pepper Sauce

"This is my own recipe for a fairly quick pasta sauce, meaning it doesn't take all day to cook. Use your own judgment when it comes to adding the spices, that's what makes it fun! Great served with angel hair pasta, fresh garlic bread, and Chianti wine."

Serving: 4

Ingredients
- 4 tablespoons olive oil
- 8 cloves crushed garlic
- 1 onion, chopped
- 1/2 (12 ounce) jar roasted red bell peppers
- 1/2 cup chopped fresh basil
- ground black pepper to taste
- 1/8 teaspoon freshly ground white pepper
- 1 pinch cayenne pepper
- 1 pinch dried sage
- 1 pinch onion powder
- 2 teaspoons dried parsley
- 2 teaspoons dried oregano
- salt to taste
- 1 tablespoon monosodium glutamate (MSG)
- 1 fluid ounce sweet vermouth (optional)
- 2 anchovy filets (optional)
- 1 (28 ounce) can Italian-style whole peeled tomatoes
- 2 (6 ounce) cans tomato paste
- 1 bay leaf

- 1/8 teaspoon fennel seed
- 1 tablespoon dried chives
- 1 cube chicken bouillon
- 3/4 pound sweet Italian sausage
- 3/4 pound spicy Italian sausage
- 2 tablespoons olive oil

Direction

- In a large saucepan sauté garlic, onion, and roasted peppers in 2 tablespoons olive oil until onions turn golden brown. Stir in fresh basil and blend well. Add ground black pepper, ground white pepper, ground red pepper, ground sage, onion powder, ground sage, onion powder, dried parsley, dried oregano, and salt. Stir until well blended. If desired, add MSG. Stir in chopped Italian tomatoes and both cans of tomato paste. Cover and simmer over medium-low heat until paste has liquefied.
- Once sauce has liquefied, add bay leaf, fennel seed, dried chives, bouillon cube, and, if desired, anchovy fillets and Vermouth. Cover and let simmer for 30 minutes. Stir occasionally.
- In a separate skillet prepare sausage by lightly browning in 2 tablespoons olive oil. Using medium heat, cover and let cook for 15 minutes. At the completion of cooking time, remove sausage from pan, and cut into 1 inch pieces. Add to sauce pot.
- Cover sauce and simmer for an additional 15 minutes. Stir occasionally and serve warm.

Nutrition Information

- Calories: 938 calories
- Total Fat: 74.5 g
- Cholesterol: 131 mg
- Sodium: 3068 mg
- Total Carbohydrate: 35.2 g
- Protein: 31.4 g

Lobster Mornay Sauce

"This recipe is very simple to make, and you can substitute crab or shrimp for the lobster. I use all three when we are craving seafood. Serve over rice or pasta."

Serving: 4 | Prep: 10 m | Cook: 20 m | Ready in: 30 m

Ingredients
- 1/4 cup butter
- 1 cup sliced fresh mushrooms
- 1 pound lobster meat, diced
- 1/4 cup all-purpose flour
- 1 cup chicken broth
- 1 cup heavy cream
- 1/2 teaspoon pepper
- 1/2 cup freshly grated Parmesan cheese

Direction

- Melt the butter in a medium saucepan over medium heat. Slowly cook and stir mushrooms in the butter until tender. Mix in lobster meat. Cook until opaque. Remove mushrooms and lobster from saucepan and set aside.
- Reduce heat to low. Place flour in pan. Cook and stir approximately 2 minutes, then stir in chicken broth,

heavy cream and pepper. Simmer 5 to 10 minutes, or until thickened.
- Stir mushrooms, lobster and Parmesan cheese into the sauce mixture. Continue cooking 5 minutes.

Nutrition Information

- Calories: 487 calories
- Total Fat: 37.6 g
- Cholesterol: 229 mg
- Sodium: 594 mg
- Total Carbohydrate: 9.8 g
- Protein: 27.8 g

Lobster Tomato Sauce

"Another one of grandma Puglia's treasures! The lobster flavor from the shell infuses into a rich and delicious tomato sauce. You may remove the lobster meat and add to the sauce or serve separately. Serve over linguine."

Serving: 6 | Prep: 20 m | Cook: 1 h 15 m | Ready in: 1 h 35 m

Ingredients
- 1/4 cup olive oil
- 1 onion, chopped
- 1 small garlic clove, crushed
- 1 tablespoon chopped fresh parsley
- 6 (6 ounce) lobster tails, thawed
- 1 (28 ounce) can crushed tomatoes

- 1 (8 ounce) can tomato sauce
- 3 tablespoons chopped fresh basil
- salt and ground black pepper to taste

Direction

- Heat olive oil in a large saucepan over medium heat.
- Cook and stir onion and garlic in hot oil until lightly browned, about 8 minutes.
- Stir parsley and lobster tails into onion and garlic; cook until shells turn bright red, 10 to 15 minutes.
- Stir crushed tomatoes, tomato sauce, basil, salt, and black pepper with lobster tails; simmer over low heat for 1 hour, stirring occasionally.
- Remove lobster tails from sauce and shake excess sauce off the shells. If desired, remove lobster meat from shells and stir into sauce or serve lobster pieces separately.

Nutrition Information

- Calories: 295 calories
- Total Fat: 13.7 g
- Cholesterol: 101 mg
- Sodium: 891 mg
- Total Carbohydrate: 15.1 g
- Protein: 29.3 g

Pantry Puttanesca

"Puttanesca is a hearty tomato sauce with a rich texture and a spicy kick. Pair it with hot pasta, and a fresh tasting, wholesome dinner will be on the table in no time."

Serving: 4 | Prep: 5 m | Cook: 16 m | Ready in: 21 m

Ingredients
- 1/3 cup olive oil
- 3 cloves garlic, minced
- 1/4 teaspoon crushed red pepper flakes, or to taste
- 1 teaspoon dried oregano
- 3 anchovy fillets, chopped, or more to taste
- 2 (15 ounce) cans diced tomatoes, drained.
- 1 (8 ounce) package spaghetti
- 1/2 cup chopped pitted kalamata olives
- 1/4 cup capers, chopped

Direction

- Fill a large pot with water. Bring to a rolling boil over high heat.
- As the water heats, pour the olive oil into a cold skillet and stir in the garlic. Turn heat to medium-low and cook and stir until the garlic is fragrant and begins to turn a golden color, 1 to 2 minutes. Stir in the red pepper flakes, oregano, and anchovies. Cook until anchovies begin to break down, about 2 minutes.
- Pour tomatoes into skillet, turn heat to medium-high, and bring sauce to a simmer. Use the back of a spoon to break down tomatoes as they cook. Simmer until sauce is reduced and combined, about 10 minutes.

- Meanwhile, cook the pasta in the boiling water. Drain when still very firm to the bite, about 9 minutes. Reserve 1/2 cup pasta water.
- Stir the olives and capers into the sauce; add pasta and toss to combine.
- Toss pasta in sauce until pasta is cooked through and well coated with sauce, about 1 minute. If sauce becomes too thick, stir in some of the reserved pasta water to thin.

Nutrition Information

- Calories: 463 calories
- Total Fat: 24 g
- Cholesterol: 3 mg
- Sodium: 945 mg
- Total Carbohydrate: 53.3 g
- Protein: 10.5 g

Pappardelle Puttanesca

"A fantastic variation of a simple but delicious Italian dish, my Puttanesca is a mildly spicy white wine tomato sauce with fresh garlic, mushrooms, capers, and anchovy-stuffed green olives. The anchovy-stuffed green olives are easy to find next to the rest of the canned olives at any major grocery store."

Serving: 8 | Prep: 20 m | Cook: 30 m | Ready in: 50 m

Ingredients
- 1/4 cup extra-virgin olive oil, or as needed
- 2 cups sliced mushrooms

- 2 tablespoons minced garlic, or to taste
- 1 cup dry white wine
- 1 (5 ounce) jar anchovy-stuffed green olives, drained and halved
- 1/4 cup capers, drained
- 2 tablespoons caper juice
- 2 (14 ounce) cans crushed tomatoes
- 1 pinch red pepper flakes, or to taste
- 1 pound dried pappardelle pasta

Direction

- Heat olive oil in a large skillet over medium-high heat. Stir in mushrooms and garlic. Cook until the mushrooms have begun to brown, about 4 minutes. Increase heat to high, and pour in wine. Bring to a boil, then stir in olives, capers, caper juice, crushed tomatoes, and pepper flakes. Return to a simmer, then reduce heat to medium-low, and cook for 20 minutes.
- Meanwhile, bring a large pot of lightly salted water to a boil. Add pasta and cook for 8 to 10 minutes or until al dente; drain and toss with sauce to serve.

Nutrition Information

- Calories: 439 calories
- Total Fat: 16.4 g
- Cholesterol: 0 mg
- Sodium: 1604 mg
- Total Carbohydrate: 53.9 g
- Protein: 11.5 g

Spicy Clam Sauce

"A very quick, simple clam sauce to serve with any light pasta. I always serve it with farfalle. This has been one of my family's favorite pasta recipes for years, and I always serve it with buttery garlic bread."

Serving: 8 | Prep: 10 m | Cook: 20 m | Ready in: 30 m

Ingredients
- 3 tablespoons olive oil
- 2 tablespoons minced garlic
- 3 (10 ounce) cans chopped clams, drained with juices reserved
- 3 tablespoons dried oregano leaves, crumbled
- ground black pepper to taste
- 1 teaspoon red pepper flakes, or to taste
- 1/2 cup grated Parmesan cheese for topping (optional)

Direction
- Heat the olive oil in a large skillet over medium-high heat. Add the garlic and drained clams; cook and stir for about 5 minutes. Season with oregano, pepper, and red pepper flakes. Pour in the reserved clam juice. Reduce heat to low, and simmer for about 20 minutes. Remove from heat and serve over pasta. Garnish with Parmesan cheese, if desired.

Nutrition Information
- Calories: 232 calories
- Total Fat: 8.8 g
- Cholesterol: 75 mg

- Sodium: 195 mg
- Total Carbohydrate: 7.7 g
- Protein: 29.1 g

Swedish Sour Cream And Caviar Sauce For Salmon

"The absolute best sauce to serve with grilled salmon, steamed artichokes, and boiled new potatoes in the summertime. Lumpfish caviar can be found in gourmet food stores or cheaper at IKEA. Wonderful with salmon, it's also great with other more mild fish dishes."

Serving: 8 | Prep: 10 m | Ready in: 10 m

Ingredients
- 1 cup sour cream
- 1 (8 ounce) container creme fraiche
- 1/2 cup mayonnaise
- 4 tablespoons chopped fresh dill
- 1 pinch white pepper
- 3 1/2 ounces red lumpfish caviar

Direction
- In a bowl, stir together sour cream, creme fraiche, mayonnaise, dill, and white pepper. Carefully mix in caviar. Cover, and refrigerate at least 1 hour before serving.

Nutrition Information
- Calories: 293 calories
- Total Fat: 30.2 g
- Cholesterol: 131 mg
- Sodium: 291 mg

- Total Carbohydrate: 3.4 g
- Protein: 5.2 g

Tuna Tomato Pasta Sauce

"Super easy to make, with ingredients everyone has hanging around in the pantry like canned tuna and canned tomatoes! Serve with about 3/4 pound of pasta, preferably penne, fusilli or macaroni, cooked according to package instructions."

Serving: 2 | Prep: 5 m | Cook: 15 m | Ready in: 20 m

Ingredients
- 2 tablespoons olive oil
- 1 small chile pepper, diced
- 1 clove garlic, minced
- 9 ounces drained canned tuna
- 3 tablespoons tomato paste
- 1 tablespoon white sugar
- 1 teaspoon salt
- 1 teaspoon ground black pepper
- 1 (22 ounce) can diced tomatoes

Direction
- Heat olive oil in a deep skillet over medium heat and cook chile and garlic until lightly browned, about 1 minute. Add tuna, tomato paste, sugar, salt, and pepper and cook for 5 minutes. Add tomatoes and simmer until flavors are well combined, 5 to 10 minutes.

Nutrition Information
- Calories: 390 calories

- Total Fat: 14.7 g
- Cholesterol: 38 mg
- Sodium: 1912 mg
- Total Carbohydrate: 24.5 g
- Protein: 36.9 g

Chapter 4: Tomato Pasta Sauces
Marinara

Allpurpose Marinara Sauce

"I use this recipe for marinara sauce as a base for all my pasta dishes. You can use the sauce 'as is' for a meatless spaghetti sauce. Or you can add just about any meat or seafood to add variety to your meals. In addition, you can add kidney beans and your favorite ingredients to make a super chili. My kids eat this pasta sauce like no other. They are happy campers when the house is filled with the aroma as this sauce is cooking."

Serving: 48 | Prep: 15 m | Cook: 40 m | Ready in: 55 m

Ingredients
- 1/4 cup olive oil
- 1 bulb garlic, cloves separated, peeled, and sliced
- 4 (28 ounce) cans whole tomatoes, chopped
- 2 (28 ounce) cans diced tomatoes
- 4 (4 ounce) cans diced green chiles
- 1 (6 ounce) can tomato paste
- 1/2 cup capers
- 1 cup pitted green olives, chopped
- 1 cup chopped fresh parsley
- 2 cups portobello mushroom caps, cut into 1/4-inch pieces
- 2 tablespoons prepared horseradish
- 1 teaspoon habanero hot sauce

- 1 tablespoon white sugar
- 1 teaspoon dried Italian seasoning
- 1 teaspoon dried oregano
- 1 teaspoon cumin

Direction

- Heat the olive oil in a large pot over medium heat, and cook the garlic until lightly browned. Drain excess oil. Mix in the whole tomatoes, diced tomatoes, green chiles, tomato paste, capers, green olives, parsley, portobello mushroom caps, horseradish, habanero sauce, and sugar. Season with Italian seasoning, oregano, and cumin. Cover, and bring to a boil. Reduce heat to low, and simmer 25 minutes.

Nutrition Information

- Calories: 41 calories
- Total Fat: 1.7 g
- Cholesterol: 0 mg
- Sodium: 400 mg
- Total Carbohydrate: 6 g
- Protein: 1.3 g

Basic Marinara For The Instant Pot

"This marinara sauce tastes like it's been simmering all day, but you'll have a savory, rich dish on the table in under an hour."

Serving: 6 | Prep: 10 m | Cook: 30 m | Ready in: 45 m

Ingredients

- 2 tablespoons olive oil
- 1 cup diced onion
- 1 tablespoon minced garlic
- 1/4 cup dry red wine
- 1 (28 ounce) can diced tomatoes
- 1 (28 ounce) can whole peeled tomatoes
- 1 tablespoon dried basil
- 1 tablespoon dried oregano
- 1 tablespoon dried parsley
- 3/4 teaspoon sea salt
- freshly ground black pepper to taste
- 1 pinch red pepper flakes
- 1 bay leaf

Direction

- Turn on a multi-functional pressure cooker (such as Instant Pot(R)) and select Sauté function to heat the pot. Add olive oil and onion; cook until onion is translucent, 3 to 5 minutes. Add garlic and cook until fragrant, about 1 minute. Pour in red wine and simmer until reduced by half.
- Pour diced tomatoes and whole tomatoes into the pot. Bring to a simmer. Stir in basil, oregano, parsley, salt, pepper, red pepper flakes, and bay leaf. Press Keep Warm. Close and lock the lid. Seal the vent. Select Manual function and set timer for 10 minutes. Allow 10 to 15 minutes for the pressure to build.
- Release pressure carefully using the quick-release method according to manufacturer's instructions,

about 5 minutes. Unlock and remove the lid. Discard bay leaf. Use an immersion blender to puree the sauce.

Nutrition Information

- Calories: 115 calories
- Total Fat: 4.8 g
- Cholesterol: 0 mg
- Sodium: 615 mg
- Total Carbohydrate: 13.8 g
- Protein: 2.8 g

Bayys Meatless Marinara From Scratch Vegan

"Serve this meatless, chunky marinara sauce from scratch with veggie-wheat pasta. You can freestyle the marinara sauce with whatever vegetables you would like to use. I also use black beans as a meat substitute for texture."

Serving: 12 | Prep: 15 m | Cook: 1 h 15 m | Ready in: 1 h 30 m

Ingredients
- 15 Roma (plum) tomatoes, diced
- 2 cups water, divided
- 1 (14.5 ounce) can diced tomatoes
- 1 (6 ounce) can tomato paste
- 2 (15 ounce) cans black beans, drained and rinsed
- 1 (8 ounce) package mushrooms, diced
- 1 green bell pepper, diced
- 1 onion, diced, or more to taste
- 1 stalk celery, chopped, or more to taste
- 2 cloves garlic, minced, or more to taste
- 2 tablespoons olive oil
- 2 tablespoons fennel seeds (optional)
- 2 cubes vegetable bouillon, or more to taste
- 2 sprigs fresh parsley, chopped
- 2 leaves fresh basil, chopped
- dried Italian seasoning to taste
- salt and ground black pepper to taste

Direction

- Combine Roma tomatoes, 1 cup water, diced tomatoes, and tomato paste in a Dutch oven over medium-low heat. Simmer for 45 minutes. Add remaining water, black beans, mushrooms, green bell pepper, onion, celery, garlic, olive oil, fennel seeds, bouillon, parsley, basil, and Italian seasoning. Simmer over low heat until thickened to desired consistency, about 45 minutes more. Season with salt and pepper.

Nutrition Information

- Calories: 133 calories
- Total Fat: 3 g
- Cholesterol: 0 mg
- Sodium: 465 mg
- Total Carbohydrate: 21.6 g
- Protein: 7 g

Best Marinara

"This is the absolute best recipe to use on tomatoes! I haven't tried it on spaghetti, but I recommend rotini or fusili. This is a marinara sauce, but better! Even my picky little sister loved it!"

Serving: 6 | Prep: 5 m | Cook: 20 m | Ready in: 25 m

Ingredients

- 2 tablespoons vegetable oil
- 1 cup chopped onion
- 2 cloves garlic, minced

- 2 stalks celery, chopped
- 1 1/2 (28 ounce) cans crushed tomatoes
- 1 (6 ounce) can tomato paste
- 2 teaspoons dried parsley
- 1 teaspoon dried basil
- 1 teaspoon dried oregano
- salt and pepper to taste

Direction

- Heat oil in large skillet over medium heat. Stir in onion, garlic and celery and cook until soft. Pour in tomatoes and tomato paste, stir, reduce heat and simmer 5 minutes. Stir in parsley, basil, oregano, salt and pepper; simmer 15 minutes, uncovered. Serve.

Nutrition Information

- Calories: 143 calories
- Total Fat: 5.4 g
- Cholesterol: 0 mg
- Sodium: 494 mg
- Total Carbohydrate: 23.5 g
- Protein: 5 g

Best Marinara Sauce Yet

"This is a very easy homemade red sauce, and the only one my 5 year old daughter will eat! Serve with your favorite pasta."

Serving: 8 | Prep: 15 m | Cook: 30 m | Ready in: 45 m

Ingredients

- 2 (14.5 ounce) cans stewed tomatoes
- 1 (6 ounce) can tomato paste
- 4 tablespoons chopped fresh parsley
- 1 clove garlic, minced
- 1 teaspoon dried oregano
- 1 teaspoon salt
- 1/4 teaspoon ground black pepper
- 6 tablespoons olive oil
- 1/3 cup finely diced onion
- 1/2 cup white wine

Direction

- In a food processor place Italian tomatoes, tomato paste, chopped parsley, minced garlic, oregano, salt, and pepper. Blend until smooth.
- In a large skillet over medium heat sauté the finely chopped onion in olive oil for 2 minutes. Add the blended tomato sauce and white wine.
- Simmer for 30 minutes, stirring occasionally.

Nutrition Information

- Calories: 151 calories
- Total Fat: 10.5 g
- Cholesterol: 0 mg
- Sodium: 685 mg
- Total Carbohydrate: 11.7 g
- Protein: 2 g

Birdmans Marinara Sauce

"Wonderful blend of vegetables and tomato sauce that can be used on any Italian dish. Use the sauce on spaghetti, in lasagna, or any other kind of Italian dish."

Serving: 10 | Prep: 15 m | Cook: 3 h 5 m | Ready in: 3 h 20 m

Ingredients
- 1 tablespoon olive oil
- 1 onion, chopped
- 3 cloves garlic, minced
- 2 (15 ounce) cans tomato sauce
- 5 tomatoes, chopped
- 12 mushrooms, sliced
- 1 small bell pepper, chopped
- 2 stalks celery, chopped
- 2 carrots, shredded
- 2 small zucchini, sliced
- 1 (6 ounce) can tomato paste
- 1/4 cup red cooking wine
- 1 tablespoon soy sauce
- 1/2 teaspoon ground black pepper
- 1 teaspoon dried basil
- 1 teaspoon dried oregano
- 1/2 teaspoon dried sage
- 2 bay leaves

Direction
- Heat olive oil in a large saucepan over medium-high heat; sauté onion and garlic until onion becomes translucent, about 5 minutes. Add tomato sauce,

tomatoes, mushrooms, bell pepper, celery, carrots, zucchini, tomato paste, cooking wine, soy sauce, and black pepper; simmer for 2 hours.
- Stir basil, oregano, sage, and bay leaves into sauce and simmer until flavors blend, 1 to 2 hours. Remove bay leaves.

Nutrition Information

- Calories: 92 calories
- Total Fat: 2 g
- Cholesterol: 0 mg
- Sodium: 724 mg
- Total Carbohydrate: 17.4 g
- Protein: 4.1 g

Chunky Marinara Sauce

"You'll love this Marinara sauce! This is great with fried eggplant or meatballs. I'm sure you could add ground meat if you wanted to make a meat sauce. "

Serving: 6 | Prep: 15 m | Cook: 20 m | Ready in: 35 m

Ingredients

- 1 tablespoon olive oil
- 1 onion, chopped
- 1 clove garlic, chopped
- 1 (14.5 ounce) can peeled and diced tomatoes
- 1 (8 ounce) can tomato sauce
- 1 teaspoon white sugar

- 1/2 teaspoon dried oregano
- 1/4 teaspoon salt

Direction

- Heat olive oil in a saucepan over medium-high heat. Add onion and garlic and cook 2 to 4 minutes until crisp-tender, stirring frequently.
- Mix in diced tomatoes, tomato sauce, sugar, oregano and salt. Bring to a boil. Reduce heat to low and simmer 15 to 20 minutes or until flavors are blended, stirring frequently.

Nutrition Information

- Calories: 54 calories
- Total Fat: 2.4 g
- Cholesterol: 0 mg
- Sodium: 443 mg
- Total Carbohydrate: 6.9 g
- Protein: 1.3 g

Easy Creamy Bell Pepper Marinara

"Add this creamy base to give a new spin to your favorite store-bought marinara."

Serving: 8 | Prep: 15 m | Cook: 20 m | Ready in: 35 m

Ingredients
- 1/4 cup butter
- 1 small onion, sliced
- 1/2 large red bell pepper, cut into matchstick-sized pieces
- 1 clove garlic, minced
- 1/4 cup all-purpose flour
- 1 cup milk
- 1/2 cup grated Parmesan cheese
- 32 ounces tomato sauce (such as Classico® Tomato and Basil Sauce)
- 1/4 teaspoon ground black pepper
- 1/2 teaspoon balsamic vinegar
- 1 dash hot sauce, or to taste
- 1 1/2 cups chopped fresh spinach

Direction

- Heat butter in a large skillet over medium heat; cook and stir onion, red bell pepper, and garlic until tender, 5 to 10 minutes. Stir in flour until dissolved and thickened, about 5 minutes. Pour in milk, stirring constantly, until well mixed. Add Parmesan cheese; stir until cheese is melted, 5 minutes.
- Stir tomato sauce into creamy onion mixture; season with black pepper, balsamic vinegar, and hot

sauce. Cook and stir until heated through, 5 to 10 minutes. Sprinkle spinach over sauce to serve.

Nutrition Information

- Calories: 138 calories
- Total Fat: 8.1 g
- Cholesterol: 22 mg
- Sodium: 725 mg
- Total Carbohydrate: 12.5 g
- Protein: 5.3 g

Easy Marinara Sauce

"We built this recipe from a lot of trial and error and a little experimentation with the wine selection. It has a sweet flavor with just a little zing to keep things interesting. Great for all types of italian dishes. We even used it for Italian sausage bombers."

Serving: 16 | Prep: 15 m | Cook: 45 m | Ready in: 1 h

Ingredients

- 3 tablespoons olive oil
- 1 Spanish onion, chopped
- 1/4 green bell pepper, chopped
- 4 cloves garlic, finely chopped
- 2 tablespoons brown sugar
- 2 teaspoons Italian seasoning
- 2 teaspoons salt
- 1 teaspoon dried oregano
- 1 teaspoon dried basil

- 1/2 teaspoon ground black pepper
- 1/4 teaspoon red pepper flakes
- 4 (14.5 ounce) cans diced tomatoes
- 1 (14 ounce) can tomato sauce
- 2 (6 ounce) cans tomato paste
- 1 cup white wine

Direction

- Heat olive oil in a large pot over medium heat; cook and stir onion, green bell pepper, and garlic until onion is translucent, 5 to 10 minutes. Add brown sugar, Italian seasoning, salt, oregano, basil, black pepper, and red pepper flakes; cook and stir until brown sugar dissolves and seasoning is fragrant, 1 to 2 minutes.
- Stir tomatoes, tomato sauce, tomato paste, and white wine into the seasoned onion mixture; bring to a boil for 10 minutes. Reduce heat and simmer, stirring occasionally, until flavors have blended, at least 30 minutes.

Nutrition Information

- Calories: 88 calories
- Total Fat: 2.9 g
- Cholesterol: 0 mg
- Sodium: 736 mg
- Total Carbohydrate: 12.8 g
- Protein: 2.2 g

Fresh Tomato Marinara Sauce

"A rich, flavorful sauce that is healthy. Great for use in pasta, lasagna, and other casseroles. My favorite way to eat it is to pour over raw zucchini 'pasta' for an extra-fresh and tasty meal that's very healthy, too! A great recipe for using up extra-ripe tomatoes from your garden. Double the batch and freeze half; it freezes well."

Serving: 6 | Prep: 15 m | Cook: 1 h 10 m | Ready in: 1 h 25 m

Ingredients
- 3 tablespoons olive oil
- 1/2 onion, chopped
- 8 large tomatoes, peeled and cut into big chunks
- 6 cloves garlic, minced
- 1 bay leaf
- 1/2 cup red wine
- 1 tablespoon honey
- 2 teaspoons dried basil
- 1 teaspoon oregano
- 1 teaspoon dried marjoram
- 1 teaspoon salt
- 1/2 teaspoon ground black pepper
- 1/4 teaspoon fennel seed
- 1/4 teaspoon crushed red pepper
- 2 teaspoons balsamic vinegar, or more to taste

Direction

- Heat olive oil in a stockpot over medium heat. Cook and stir onion in hot oil until softened, about 5 minutes; add tomatoes, garlic, and bay leaf. Bring the liquid from the tomatoes to a boil, reduce to medium-low, and simmer mixture until tomatoes are softened, about 30 minutes.
- Stir red wine, honey, basil, oregano, marjoram, salt, black pepper, fennel seed, and crushed red pepper into the tomato mixture; bring again to a simmer and cook until herbs have flavored the sauce, about 30 minutes more.
- Stir balsamic vinegar into the sauce.

Nutrition Information

- Calories: 147 calories
- Total Fat: 7.4 g
- Cholesterol: 0 mg
- Sodium: 403 mg
- Total Carbohydrate: 16.5 g
- Protein: 2.7 g

Hidden Veggie Marinara Sauce For Kids

"I have young boys and they are, unfortunately, picky eaters. However, when I make this marinara sauce, and then blend it up so no veggies can be picked out, they love it. I also use this for pizza sauce, lasagna, and any recipe that calls for marinara. I hope your family enjoys as much as we do!"

Serving: 6 | Prep: 20 m | Cook: 1 h 10 m | Ready in: 1 h 30 m

Ingredients
- 2 tablespoons olive oil
- 1 small onion, diced
- 2 garlic cloves, minced
- 1 (32 ounce) can diced tomatoes
- 1 large carrot, finely shredded
- 1 stalk celery, diced
- 2 teaspoons Italian seasoning
- 1 teaspoon dried oregano
- 1/2 teaspoon salt
- 1/8 teaspoon ground black pepper
- 1 bay leaf

Direction
- Heat olive oil in a saucepan over medium-low heat. Cook and stir onion in the hot oil until translucent, about 10 minutes. Add garlic; cook and stir until fragrant, about 30 seconds.
- Stir diced tomatoes, carrot, celery, Italian seasoning, oregano, salt, pepper, and bay leaf into the saucepan. Simmer until flavors combine, about 1 hour.
- Pour sauce into a food processor, discarding bay leaf. Cover and blend carefully until smooth.

Nutrition Information
- Calories: 86 calories
- Total Fat: 4.6 g

- Cholesterol: 0 mg
- Sodium: 446 mg
- Total Carbohydrate: 8.3 g
- Protein: 1.7 g

Marinara Sauce I

"This is a delicious simple sauce which goes with anything. You can have it plain over pasta or make lasagna with it. You can make ziti or spaghetti and meatballs (just cook the meatballs in the sauce - it will take longer) or anything you can think of. It makes good, slightly too bland, pizza sauce. You can triple the batch and freeze it in jars."

Serving: 4 | Prep: 15 m | Cook: 15 m | Ready in: 30 m

Ingredients
- 2 (28 ounce) cans whole peeled tomatoes
- 1 (6 ounce) can tomato paste
- 4 tablespoons olive oil
- 4 cloves garlic, minced
- 1/4 cup chopped fresh parsley
- 1/2 tablespoon salt
- 1/2 cup red wine

Direction
- In a medium bowl, blend the whole tomatoes and paste; reserve.
- In a large saucepan, warm olive oil over medium-low heat and add garlic; cook for a few minutes, but make sure to not brown the garlic.

- Pour tomato mixture in saucepan and stir; cook over medium heat for 10 minutes. Add parsley, salt and wine; reduce heat to low and simmer, stirring occasionally, until sauce thickens; serve.

Nutrition Information
- Calories: 252 calories
- Total Fat: 14.3 g
- Cholesterol: 0 mg
- Sodium: 1772 mg
- Total Carbohydrate: 25.7 g
- Protein: 5.2 g

Marinara Sauce Ii

"Marinara sauce that is great on any type of pasta."

Serving: 6 | Prep: 15 m | Cook: 20 m | Ready in: 35 m

Ingredients
- 4 tablespoons olive oil
- 4 cloves garlic, minced
- 1 small onion, chopped
- 1 (28 ounce) can whole peeled tomatoes
- 1 (28 ounce) can crushed tomatoes
- 3 teaspoons dried basil leaves
- 1 teaspoon white sugar
- salt and pepper to taste

Direction
- In a skillet over medium heat, sauté garlic and onion in the olive oil; about 10 minutes. Break apart the

whole tomatoes with your hands and add to the pan along with the crushed tomatoes, basil, sugar, salt and pepper. Cover and simmer 20 minutes, stirring occasionally.

Nutrition Information

- Calories: 156 calories
- Total Fat: 9.6 g
- Cholesterol: 0 mg
- Sodium: 360 mg
- Total Carbohydrate: 17.5 g
- Protein: 3.6 g

Marinara Sauce Iii

"Here is a rich and hearty tomato sauce which does not need sugar or butter to cut the acidity from the tomato. Olive oil is optional for those watching their waistlines."

Serving: 5 | Prep: 20 m | Cook: 3 h | Ready in: 3 h 20 m

Ingredients
- 1/2 cup diced onion
- 3 cloves garlic, minced
- 1 (28 ounce) can peeled and diced tomatoes
- 1/3 cup shredded carrot
- 1/3 cup chopped celery
- 1/4 cup shredded red bell pepper
- 1 cup chopped fresh mushrooms
- 1 tablespoon dried oregano
- 2 tablespoons dried parsley
- 1 tablespoon dried basil leaves
- 1/2 cup extra virgin olive oil

Direction
- In a saucepan sauté onion and garlic over medium-low heat until they start to become clear. Combine in a pot, diced tomatoes, carrots, celery, red bell pepper, mushrooms, oregano, parsley, basil and olive oil. Bring to boil and reduce heat to medium-low. Simmer for at least 1 hour, however, 3 hours of cooking develops better flavor and consistency.

Nutrition Information
- Calories: 259 calories

- Total Fat: 22.7 g
- Cholesterol: 0 mg
- Sodium: 260 mg
- Total Carbohydrate: 10.5 g
- Protein: 2.4 g

Marinara With White Wine

"This is a rich marinara with white wine and anchovies. It's rather soupy, so simmer it as long as it takes to reach your desired consistency."

Serving: 10 | Prep: 25 m | Cook: 1 h 15 m | Ready in: 1 h 40 m

Ingredients
- 1 tablespoon olive oil from anchovies
- 2 tablespoons minced garlic
- 1/2 cup chopped onion
- 1 green bell pepper, chopped
- 1/2 cup white wine
- 1 1/2 pounds grape tomatoes
- 1 (15 ounce) can stewed tomatoes, with juice
- 6 anchovy fillets
- 1/2 teaspoon salt
- black pepper to taste
- 1/2 teaspoon dried basil
- 1 teaspoon chopped parsley
- 1/2 teaspoon dried oregano
- 1 small bay leaf

Direction

- Heat the anchovy oil in a saucepan over medium heat, stir in garlic, onions, and green pepper; cook for a few minutes until the onion softens and turns translucent. Pour in the wine, and simmer until reduced by half. Meanwhile, place the grape tomatoes, stewed tomatoes, and anchovies into the bowl of a blender; puree until smooth.
- Season with salt, pepper, basil, parsley, oregano, and bay leaf. Bring to a simmer over medium-high heat, then reduce heat to medium-low and simmer for 1 hour. Season to taste with salt and pepper before serving.

Nutrition Information

- Calories: 61 calories
- Total Fat: 1.9 g
- Cholesterol: 2 mg
- Sodium: 305 mg
- Total Carbohydrate: 8.1 g
- Protein: 2 g

Millers Marinara

"Best if cooked in slow cooker for several hours, but can be done in as little as two on the stove. May be frozen for use later. Really great over Chicken Parmesan. Also works for vegetarians!"

Serving: 12 | Prep: 15 m | Cook: 8 h 5 m | Ready in: 8 h 20 m

Ingredients

- 1/4 cup canola oil
- 1 medium onion, chopped
- 1 (28 ounce) can crushed tomatoes
- 1 (8 ounce) can tomato sauce
- 1 (10.75 ounce) can tomato puree
- 2 1/2 tablespoons garlic powder
- 2 tablespoons dried oregano
- 2 tablespoons dried basil
- 2 tablespoons salt
- 2 tablespoons white sugar
- 2 teaspoons ground black pepper

Direction

- Heat the canola oil in a skillet over medium heat, and sauté the onion until tender.
- In a slow cooker, mix the onion and remaining oil, crushed tomatoes, tomato sauce, tomato puree, garlic powder, oregano, basil, salt, sugar, and pepper.
- Cover slow cooker, and cook sauce 8 hours on Low.

Nutrition Information

- Calories: 98 calories
- Total Fat: 5.1 g
- Cholesterol: 0 mg
- Sodium: 1448 mg
- Total Carbohydrate: 13.1 g
- Protein: 2.4 g

Mommas Marinara Sauce

"This is a very good quality marinara sauce to serve with any pasta dish. Our family has loved it for years. The hint to a good marinara sauce is cooking for an extended period of time over low heat."

Serving: 5

Ingredients
- 1 (28 ounce) jar spaghetti sauce
- 1 (14.5 ounce) can peeled and diced tomatoes
- 1 (14.5 ounce) can stewed tomatoes
- 1 (6 ounce) can tomato paste
- 1 onion, chopped
- 2 teaspoons minced garlic
- 1 teaspoon dried thyme

Direction
- Combine all ingredients, and cook for at least 3-4 hours before serving.

Nutrition Information
- Calories: 213 calories
- Total Fat: 4.6 g
- Cholesterol: 3 mg
- Sodium: 1220 mg
- Total Carbohydrate: 38.3 g
- Protein: 6 g

Rustic Marinara Sauce

"I've been perfecting this recipe for over 10 years. Melting just a little cheese in the sauce adds great richness without overwhelming the tomatoes. And it's easy to keep these ingredients stocked in the house! Makes for amazing leftovers!"

Serving: 6 | Prep: 15 m | Cook: 1 h 15 m | Ready in: 1 h 30 m

Ingredients
- 1/2 cup olive oil
- 2 white onions, diced
- 8 cloves garlic, minced
- 1 (28 ounce) can petite diced tomatoes
- 1 (28 ounce) can diced tomatoes
- 1 cup dry white wine
- 1 (6 ounce) can tomato paste
- 1 tablespoon dried oregano
- 1/2 teaspoon salt
- 1/2 teaspoon white sugar
- 1/2 teaspoon ground black pepper
- 1/4 teaspoon red pepper flakes
- 3 bay leaves
- 1 cup freshly grated Pecorino-Romano cheese, divided
- 3/4 cup chopped fresh basil
- 1/2 cup chopped fresh parsley

Direction
- Heat olive oil in a large Dutch oven or heavy pot over medium heat; cook and stir onions for 5 minutes. Add garlic and cook, stirring occasionally, until onions are translucent, about 5 minutes more.

- Mix petite diced tomatoes, diced tomatoes, white wine, tomato paste, oregano, salt, sugar, black pepper, red pepper flakes, and bay leaves into onion mixture; reduce heat to low, cover Dutch oven, and simmer, stirring occasionally, until flavors blend, about 1 hour.
- Remove Dutch oven from heat. Add 1/2 cup Pecorino-Romano cheese, basil, and parsley into sauce; stir until cheese melts, about 5 minutes. Discard bay leaves. Sprinkle remaining cheese over sauce when serving.

Nutrition Information

- Calories: 332 calories
- Total Fat: 20.4 g
- Cholesterol: 7 mg
- Sodium: 956 mg
- Total Carbohydrate: 21.4 g
- Protein: 7.2 g

Simple Marinara Sauce

"This is a simple marinara sauce, good over any pasta or on lasagna."

Serving: 8 | Prep: 10 m | Cook: 40 m | Ready in: 50 m

Ingredients
- 2 tablespoons olive oil
- 3 cloves garlic, minced
- 1 (28 ounce) can crushed tomatoes
- 1 (28 ounce) can tomato puree

- 2 1/2 tablespoons dried oregano
- 2 1/2 tablespoons dried parsley
- 1/4 cup grated Romano cheese
- 1/3 cup grated Parmesan cheese
- 2 bay leaves
- 1 teaspoon onion powder

Direction

- Heat oil in a large saucepan over medium heat. Sauté garlic until aromatic and tender. Stir in crushed tomatoes, tomato puree, oregano, parsley, Romano cheese, Parmesan cheese, bay leaves and onion powder. Reduce heat to low and simmer for at least 40 minutes.

Nutrition Information

- Calories: 135 calories
- Total Fat: 6 g
- Cholesterol: 7 mg
- Sodium: 619 mg
- Total Carbohydrate: 18 g
- Protein: 6 g

Slow Cooker Spinach Marinara Sauce

"Veggie packed pasta sauce prepared in the slow cooker! Note -- this is a very sweet and spicy tomato sauce so adjust the seasonings (salt, pepper and garlic) to suit your taste!"

Serving: 8 | Prep: 15 m | Cook: 5 h | Ready in: 5 h 15 m

Ingredients
- 1/4 cup olive oil
- 1 onion, chopped
- 5 cloves garlic, minced
- 1/3 cup grated carrot
- 1 (10 ounce) package frozen chopped spinach, thawed and drained
- 2 2/3 (6 ounce) cans tomato paste
- 1 (4.5 ounce) can sliced mushrooms, drained
- 2 tablespoons salt
- 2 tablespoons dried oregano
- 2 tablespoons dried basil
- 2 1/2 tablespoons crushed red pepper
- 2 bay leaves
- 1 (28 ounce) can peeled and crushed tomatoes, with liquid

Direction
- In a 5 quart slow cooker, combine olive oil, onion, garlic, carrot, spinach, tomato paste, mushrooms, salt, oregano, basil, crushed red pepper, bay leaves and tomatoes.
- Cover and cook on high for 4 hours. Stir, reduce heat to low and cook for 1 to 2 hours more.

Nutrition Information
- Calories: 176 calories
- Total Fat: 8.2 g
- Cholesterol: 0 mg
- Sodium: 2418 mg
- Total Carbohydrate: 25.1 g

- Protein: 6.6 g

Tomato Harvest Marinara Sauce

"Fresh-tasting Italian-style marinara sauce is a winter luxury. It's a process to make this canned version, but oh, so worth it! Follow canning protocol to prepare this cooking staple you'll love finding in your pantry in January. Vary the amounts of garlic and spices according to your family's taste. Use this as a base sauce and add sausage, ground turkey, and other spices."

Serving: 40 | Prep: 1 h | Cook: 4 h | Ready in: 5 h

Ingredients
- 25 pounds plum tomatoes, cored and halved lengthwise
- 3 bay leaves
- 1 1/2 tablespoons honey
- 1 tablespoon dried oregano
- 1 tablespoon salt
- 2 teaspoons ground black pepper
- 1/2 cup extra-virgin olive oil
- 1 pound yellow onions, finely chopped
- 10 cloves garlic, finely chopped
- 10 1-quart canning jars with rings and lids
- 10 teaspoons salt, divided
- 1 3/4 cups bottled lemon juice, divided

Direction

- Place tomatoes, bay leaves, honey, oregano, 1 tablespoon salt, and black pepper in a large stockpot and cover with water. Stir to combine, cover, and bring to a low boil over medium-high heat. Remove cover and simmer 20 minutes, stirring occasionally. Remove bay leaves. Taste and adjust seasoning.
- Heat olive oil in a large skillet over medium-high heat. Cook and stir onions and garlic in the hot oil until the onions are softened but not browned, about 10 minutes.
- Transfer the cooked tomatoes to a food mill placed over a bowl and puree in batches, separating the tomato pulp and juice from the tomato skins and seeds. Return the tomato pulp and juice to the stockpot, add the cooked onions and garlic, and cook, uncovered, over medium-high heat until sauce thickens and reduces by about half, about 1 to 1-1/2 hours. Stir occasionally to prevent scorching.
- Prepare quart jars, rings, and lids by heating them in boiling water in a canning kettle for at least 5 minutes. When the sauce is ready, remove jars and lids and place on dry towel.
- To each jar, add 1 teaspoon salt and 3 tablespoons bottled lemon juice. Ladle the hot tomato sauce into jars, leaving 1/2-inch of space at the top of each jar. Wipe jar rims with a clean, damp cloth, place lids onto jars, and screw on rings.

- Place filled jars in the canning kettle. Return water to a simmer, adding more water if needed to cover the jars by at least 1/2 inch. Cover kettle and bring water to a boil. Cook at a steady boil to process the jars until fully sealed, about 45 minutes. Turn off heat and let jars rest 5 minutes before removing and cooling on a clean, dry towel placed on kitchen counter or table. Check that the lids have sealed, and store in a cool, dark place for up to 1 year.

Nutrition Information
- Calories: 87 calories
- Total Fat: 3.4 g
- Cholesterol: 0 mg
- Sodium: 773 mg
- Total Carbohydrate: 13.9 g
- Protein: 2.7 g

Worlds Best Marinara

"The only marinara you'll ever need! Serve with your favorite pasta."

Serving: 8 | Prep: 15 m | Cook: 40 m | Ready in: 55 m

Ingredients
- 1 tablespoon olive oil
- 1 sweet onion, diced
- 4 cloves garlic, minced
- 1 (8 ounce) package fresh mushrooms, chopped
- 1 red bell pepper, diced
- 1 cup fresh flat-leaf parsley, torn

- 2 tablespoons oregano
- 2 tablespoons white sugar
- 2 teaspoons dried basil
- 1 teaspoon dried rosemary
- 1/2 teaspoon dried sage
- 1/2 teaspoon red pepper flakes
- 1/2 teaspoon salt
- ground black pepper to taste
- 1 (28 ounce) can tomato sauce

Direction

- Heat olive oil in a saucepan over medium heat; cook and stir onion and garlic until fragrant, about 2 minutes. Add mushrooms, red bell pepper, and parsley; cook and stir until mushrooms are slightly softened, about 2 minutes. Add oregano, sugar, basil, rosemary, sage, red pepper flakes, salt, and black pepper; stir to combine, 2 minutes.
- Stir tomato sauce into seasoned onion-mushroom mixture; cook over low heat until flavors have combined, 30 minutes.
- Transfer half the sauce to a blender; blend until smooth. Return to saucepan with the remaining sauce; stir to combine.

Nutrition Information

- Calories: 75 calories
- Total Fat: 2.2 g
- Cholesterol: 0 mg
- Sodium: 666 mg
- Total Carbohydrate: 13 g

- Protein: 2.9 g

Tasty Tomato Sauces

All Day Versatile Sauce

"I have found that cooking your sauce all day like my father taught me is the best way. In addition to that, I make my sauce this way whether I am making linguine, stuffed shells or lasagna. I like to utilize convenience whenever possible so I use pre minced and jarred herbs. You can use what ever your preference is for meat, whether it be ground turkey meatballs or chicken Italian sausage. It will always be a hit with your family and friends! Try serving with your favorite pasta."

Serving: 6

Ingredients
- 1 tablespoon olive oil
- 1 large onion, chopped
- 3 cloves garlic, minced
- 1 teaspoon dried oregano
- 2 teaspoons dried basil
- 1/2 pound beef neck bones
- 1 (29 ounce) can tomato sauce
- 1 (14.5 ounce) can stewed tomatoes
- 2 (6 ounce) cans tomato paste
- 3 cups water
- 1 pound lean ground beef

Direction

- In a large pot sauté onion, garlic, oregano and basil in 1 tablespoon of olive oil. Add the neck bones and let simmer with the lid on until the onions are transparent. Note: if using ground beef cook with onion mixture.
- Once onions are clear, add the tomato sauce, tomatoes, tomato paste and water. If using meat in your recipe add at this time. Cover and simmer for several hours.
- Before serving, remove neck bones and discard.

Nutrition Information

- Calories: 330 calories
- Total Fat: 18.6 g
- Cholesterol: 57 mg
- Sodium: 1360 mg
- Total Carbohydrate: 25.3 g
- Protein: 18.7 g

Amazing Ground Turkey Tomato Sauce

"This is my tried and true best pasta sauce that is both fresh and healthy!"

Serving: 4 | Prep: 15 m | Cook: 40 m | Ready in: 55 m

Ingredients

- 1/4 cup olive oil
- 1/2 white onion, chopped
- 1 tomato, chopped

- 6 basil leaves, chopped
- 4 cloves garlic, minced
- 1 (20 ounce) package ground turkey
- 1 teaspoon Italian seasoning
- 1/4 teaspoon oregano
- 2 (15 ounce) cans tomato sauce
- 1/2 (6 ounce) can tomato paste, or to taste
- salt and ground black pepper to taste

Direction

- Heat olive oil in a large pot over medium-high heat. Sauté onion, tomato, basil, and garlic in hot oil until the onion begins to soften, about 5 minutes.
- Break ground turkey into small pieces and add to pot; season with Italian seasoning and oregano. Cook and stir mixture until turkey is completely browned, 7 to 10 minutes.
- Stir tomato sauce into the turkey mixture; bring to a boil, reduce heat to low, and simmer until the sauce has thickened slightly, 20 to 25 minutes.
- Stir tomato paste into the turkey mixture until evenly colored; season with salt and pepper. Cook until the liquid is reheated, 1 to 2 minutes more.

Nutrition Information

- Calories: 413 calories
- Total Fat: 24.8 g
- Cholesterol: 105 mg
- Sodium: 1352 mg
- Total Carbohydrate: 19.4 g
- Protein: 32.5 g

Amazingly Simple Tomato Sauce

"I've used this sauce for lasagna, ziti, eggplant Parmesan, meatballs, and spaghetti. You name it, it's great with it."

Serving: 10 | Prep: 10 m | Cook: 1 h 5 m | Ready in: 1 h 15 m

Ingredients
- 2 teaspoons olive oil
- 1/2 cup minced onion
- 2 cloves garlic, crushed
- 1 (28 ounce) can crushed tomatoes
- 2 (6.5 ounce) cans canned tomato sauce
- 2 (6 ounce) cans tomato paste
- 1/2 cup water
- 2 tablespoons white sugar
- 2 tablespoons chopped fresh parsley
- 1 1/2 teaspoons dried basil
- 1 tablespoon salt
- 1 teaspoon Italian seasoning
- 1/2 teaspoon fennel seeds
- 1/4 teaspoon ground black pepper

Direction
- Heat olive oil in a large, heavy pot over medium heat. Cook and stir onion and garlic in hot oil until tender, 5 to 7 minutes.

- Stir crushed tomatoes, tomato sauce, tomato paste, and water with the onion mixture until smooth; add sugar, parsley, basil, salt, Italian seasoning, fennel, and pepper. Stir the mixture, bring to a simmer, reduce heat to low, and cook, stirring occasionally, until thickened and the seasonings have permeated the sauce, 1 hour to 90 minutes.

Nutrition Information
- Calories: 86 calories
- Total Fat: 1.4 g
- Cholesterol: 0 mg
- Sodium: 1265 mg
- Total Carbohydrate: 17.9 g
- Protein: 3.5 g

Asparagus Mousse

"Try this asparagus hollandaise topping for grilled chicken and rice."

Serving: 6 | Prep: 15 m | Cook: 7 m | Ready in: 22 m

Ingredients
- 1 pound asparagus, cut into 1/2-inch pieces
- 3 green onions, cut into 1/2-inch pieces
- 4 egg yolks
- 2 tablespoons fresh lemon juice
- 1/4 teaspoon salt
- 1/4 teaspoon Tabasco sauce

- 1 cup hot melted butter

Direction

- Bring a large pot of lightly salted water to a boil. Add the asparagus and green onions; cook 5 to 7 minutes, or until asparagus is tender. Strain through a mesh strainer, and press out excess water. Place into the bowl of a blender and puree until smooth, then pour into a bowl and set aside.
- Rinse out the blender bowl, then add the egg yolks, lemon juice, salt, and Tabasco sauce. Cover, leaving the hole in the lid open, and blend for about 5 seconds. Continue to blend at high speed while pouring the butter in a thin stream though the hole in the lid. Turn the blender off once all the butter has been added and the sauce has thickened. Pour into the asparagus puree and fold until evenly blended. Serve immediately.

Nutrition Information

- Calories: 325 calories
- Total Fat: 33.7 g
- Cholesterol: 218 mg
- Sodium: 324 mg
- Total Carbohydrate: 4.3 g
- Protein: 3.9 g

Basic Creole Sauce

"I cook a big batch of this sauce and keep in the freezer for when I need to pull together a quick dinner party or supper for my family. Just reheat and add a combination of shrimp, sausage, or chicken and serve over hot rice. Add in a combination of the optional ingredients to make it your own. You will have a meal fit for company."

Serving: 24 | Prep: 45 m | Cook: 1 h | Ready in: 2 h 15 m

Ingredients
- 2 tablespoons olive oil
- 2 cups chopped celery
- 2 cups chopped onion
- 2 cups chopped green bell pepper
- 2 cups chopped carrot
- 6 cloves garlic, chopped
- 4 (14.5 ounce) cans whole peeled tomatoes with liquid, chopped
- 4 cups water
- 2 tablespoons chicken bouillon granules
- 2 bay leaves
- 1 tablespoon red pepper flakes (optional)
- 1 tablespoon smoked paprika (optional)
- 1 pinch saffron (optional)
- 1 pinch dried oregano, or to taste (optional)
- 1 pinch dried basil, or to taste (optional)
- 1 pinch dried thyme, or to taste (optional)

- 1 orange, zested (optional)
- 1 (8 ounce) bottle clam juice (optional)
- 1 cup white wine (optional)
- salt and ground black pepper to taste
- 6 1-pint canning jars with lids and rings

Direction

- Heat olive oil in a large pot over medium heat. Stir in celery, onion, green bell pepper, carrot, and garlic; cook and stir until the vegetables are tender, about 10 minutes.
- Stir tomatoes with their juice, water, chicken bouillon cubes, and bay leaves into the vegetable mixture.
- Stir in red pepper flakes, smoked paprika, saffron, oregano, basil, thyme, orange zest, clam juice, and white wine.
- Bring the sauce to a boil, reduce heat to low, and simmer until the flavors have blended, at least 1 hour. Season to taste with salt and black pepper.
- Allow the sauce to cool completely.
- To store, pour into pint glass canning jars, cover with lids and rings, and place into freezer. Sauce can be frozen up to 3 months before using.

Nutrition Information

- Calories: 49 calories
- Total Fat: 1.5 g
- Cholesterol: < 1 mg
- Sodium: 229 mg
- Total Carbohydrate: 6.9 g

- Protein: 1.2 g

Basic Sauce For Pasta

"This is a basic mild pasta sauce my mother made for years and is still a family favorite. You can add browned ground beef, mushrooms, grated carrots, zucchini or other veggies. We especially like mushrooms or ground beef. It's easy and quick but as with most things like this, the longer and slower it simmers the better it tastes."

Serving: 4 | Prep: 15 m | Cook: 30 m | Ready in: 45 m

Ingredients
- 1 tablespoon olive oil
- 1 onion, finely chopped
- 1 clove garlic, minced
- 2 (8 ounce) cans tomato sauce
- 1 teaspoon dried oregano
- salt and pepper to taste
- 1 tablespoon processed cheese sauce
- 1 cup water

Direction
- In a large skillet over medium heat, sauté' onion and garlic in the olive oil for about 5 minutes. Add tomato sauce, oregano, salt, pepper, cheese sauce and water. Lower heat and simmer until it thickens; about 30 minutes.

Nutrition Information

- Calories: 82 calories
- Total Fat: 4.5 g
- Cholesterol: 3 mg
- Sodium: 651 mg
- Total Carbohydrate: 9.7 g
- Protein: 2.4 g

Bayys Natural Veggie Chunky Meat Sauce

"A healthy clean vegetable chunky meat sauce. Made from scratch and simmered low for 2 hours. Full of antioxidants, vitamins and minerals. Serve over spaghetti."

Serving: 10 | Prep: 40 m | Cook: 1 h 52 m | Ready in: 2 h 32 m

Ingredients
- 12 fresh red plum tomatoes, chopped
- 1 cup vegetable stock
- 2 green bell peppers, chopped
- 1 (6 ounce) can tomato paste
- 8 small mushrooms, chopped
- 1/4 cup distilled white vinegar
- 1/4 cup olive oil
- 1 pound lean ground beef
- 1 large onion, chopped
- 1 bunch fresh parsley, chopped
- 1 shallot, chopped
- 9 cloves garlic, minced
- 2 habanero peppers, chopped

- 2 tablespoons Italian seasoning
- 2 teaspoons fennel seeds
- 1 teaspoon white sugar
- 3 leaves fresh basil, chopped

Direction

- Place chopped plum tomatoes in a food processor; pulse until pureed. Transfer to a Dutch oven over medium heat. Add vegetable stock, green bell peppers, tomato paste, mushrooms, vinegar, and oil. Bring to a boil; reduce heat and simmer until saucy, 1 1/2 to 2 hours.
- Heat a large skillet over medium-high heat. Cook and stir ground beef in the hot skillet until browned and crumbly, 5 to 7 minutes. Drain and discard grease. Transfer cooked beef to the Dutch oven.
- Place onion, parsley, shallot, garlic, habanero peppers, Italian seasoning, fennel seeds, sugar, and basil into the Dutch oven. Cover and continue to simmer until vegetables are tender, 12 to 15 minutes more.

Nutrition Information

- Calories: 194 calories
- Total Fat: 11.5 g
- Cholesterol: 32 mg
- Sodium: 219 mg
- Total Carbohydrate: 12.8 g
- Protein: 11.6 g

Best Spaghetti Sauce In The World

"Fresh and soooo tasteful, you'll love it! Vermouth and chicken stock add depth of flavor."

Serving: 4 | Prep: 10 m | Cook: 15 m | Ready in: 25 m

Ingredients
- 3 tablespoons butter
- 1 teaspoon minced garlic
- 16 roma (plum) tomatoes, chopped
- 1/2 cup chicken stock
- 1/3 cup dry vermouth
- 2 tablespoons fresh basil, chopped

Direction
- In a large saucepan, melt butter over low heat. Toss in garlic and sauté 1 to 2 minutes, until slightly golden. Mix chopped tomatoes into pan. Stir in chicken stock, thinning with 1 to 2 tablespoons water if necessary. Cook over medium heat until bubbly. Stir in Vermouth and cook 5 minutes more. Mix in basil just before serving.

Nutrition Information
- Calories: 156 calories
- Total Fat: 9.2 g
- Cholesterol: 24 mg
- Sodium: 196 mg
- Total Carbohydrate: 12.9 g
- Protein: 2.5 g

Best Vodka Sauce

"Friends will think they are in a five-star restaurant and that you slaved for hours. That'll be our secret."

Serving: 16 | Prep: 10 m | Cook: 15 m | Ready in: 25 m

Ingredients
- 2 tablespoons minced garlic
- 1/2 cup vodka (such as Ciroc®)
- 1 pint heavy whipping cream
- 1 (28 ounce) jar tomato sauce
- 1 (16 ounce) can crushed tomatoes
- 1/2 cup freshly grated Parmesan cheese
- 1 tablespoon chopped fresh basil
- 1 tablespoon chopped fresh parsley

Direction
- Heat a large saucepan over high heat until the surface is very hot; add minced garlic and sear until brown, 1 to 2 minutes. Pour vodka into the saucepan, taking care to avoid any flames that ignite from the alcohol meeting the hot surface of the pan. Quickly pour cream into pan to douse the flames and stir; add tomato sauce, crushed tomatoes, Parmesan cheese, basil, and parsley.
- Bring the mixture to a boil, remove from heat, and rest sauce long enough to let herbs flavor the sauce, 5 to 10 minutes.

Nutrition Information
- Calories: 153 calories
- Total Fat: 11.9 g

- Cholesterol: 43 mg
- Sodium: 344 mg
- Total Carbohydrate: 6 g
- Protein: 2.8 g

Big Pot Sauce

"Slow cooked sugo (spaghetti sauce) just like Nonna's."

Serving: 80 | Prep: 1 h | Cook: 3 h | Ready in: 4 h

Ingredients
- 1 large diced onion
- 20 cloves garlic
- 1/2 cup olive oil
- 1 tablespoon crushed red pepper
- 2 (4 ounce) links hot Italian sausage
- 1 cup dried oregano
- 1/4 cup dried basil
- 7 (28 ounce) cans whole peeled tomatoes
- 1 cup red wine

Direction
- In a medium skillet, cook sausages over medium heat until juices run clear. Drain, and cut into bite sized pieces. Set aside.
- In large (13 quart) stock pot over medium heat, sauté onion, garlic and crushed red pepper in olive oil until golden brown. Stir in sausage pieces, half the oregano and half the basil, and cook 10 minutes. Stir in the tomatoes, increase the heat to high and bring to a boil.

- Stir in the remaining oregano and basil, reduce heat to low, and simmer 90 minutes, stirring occasionally.
- Pour in the red wine, and with a handheld mixer, carefully blend the sauce in the pot until the tomatoes have been chopped into small pieces and the sauce is thick and chunky. Serve.

Nutrition Information

- Calories: 38 calories
- Total Fat: 2.1 g
- Cholesterol: 1 mg
- Sodium: 122 mg
- Total Carbohydrate: 4.1 g
- Protein: 1.1 g

Bloody Mary Sauce

"Flavorful way of having a Bloody Mary! Jar and store in the refrigerator for up to 7 days."

Serving: 8 | Prep: 15 m | Cook: 13 m | Ready in: 28 m

Ingredients
- 1 red onion, chopped
- 2 stalks celery, chopped
- 2 cloves garlic, chopped
- salt and ground black pepper to taste
- 1 (14.5 ounce) can diced tomatoes
- 2 fluid ounces vodka
- 1 lemon, juiced
- hot sauce

- 1 dash Worcestershire sauce

Direction

- Heat a skillet over medium heat. Add onion, celery, garlic, salt, and pepper. Cook and stir until slightly softened, about 3 minutes. Add diced tomatoes, vodka, lemon juice, hot sauce, and Worcestershire sauce. Bring to a simmer. Cook until sauce is hot and flavors are combined, about 5 minutes.
- Fill blender halfway with sauce. Cover and hold lid down with a potholder; pulse a few times before leaving on to blend. Pour into a lidded jar or container. Repeat with remaining sauce.

Nutrition Information

- Calories: 38 calories
- Total Fat: 0.1 g
- Cholesterol: 0 mg
- Sodium: 112 mg
- Total Carbohydrate: 5 g
- Protein: 0.9 g

Bottled Spaghetti Sauce

"My friend came over today and we bottled this fabulous spaghetti sauce! I'm so excited to have it all year long! Store in a cool, dark area."

Serving: 112 | Prep: 1 h | Cook: 3 h 5 m | Ready in: 1 d 4 h 5 m

Ingredients

- 39 pounds fresh tomatoes, halved
- 3 pounds onions, halved
- 2 heads garlic cloves, peeled
- 2 cups olive oil
- 1 cup white sugar
- 1/2 cup salt
- 2 tablespoons dried oregano
- 1 tablespoon dried basil
- 6 (6 ounce) cans tomato paste, or as needed

Direction

- Bring a large pot of water to a boil. Add fourteen 1-quart jars; simmer to sterilize. Wash lids and rings in warm soapy water.
- Puree tomatoes in batches in a blender until smooth. Pour into a large pot. Add onions and garlic to the blender; puree until smooth. Mix into the pot.
- Stir olive oil, sugar, salt, oregano, and basil into the pot; bring to a boil. Stir in tomato paste. Simmer sauce, adding more tomato paste if needed, until thickened, about 2 hours.
- Pack sauce into hot, sterilized jars, filling to within 1/4 inch of the top. Wipe the rims of the jars with a moist paper towel to remove any food residue. Top with lids and screw on rings.
- Place a rack in the bottom of a large stockpot and fill halfway with water. Bring to a boil and lower jars 2 inches apart into the boiling water using a holder. Pour in more boiling water if necessary to bring the

water level to at least 1 inch above the tops of the jars. Bring the water to a rolling boil, cover the pot, and process for 45 minutes.
- Remove the jars from the stockpot and place onto a cloth-covered or wood surface, several inches apart, until cool, at least 24 hours. Press the top of each lid with a finger, ensuring that the seal is tight (lid does not move up or down at all).

Nutrition Information
- Calories: 84 calories
- Total Fat: 4.2 g
- Cholesterol: 0 mg
- Sodium: 81 mg
- Total Carbohydrate: 11.2 g
- Protein: 2 g

Bryans Sweet And Hot Tomato Pasta Sauce

"A tomato sauce that is sweet at the first bite then fades to hot. A delicious recipe that can be used as a base for your own mixture of vegetables."

Serving: 4 | Prep: 15 m | Cook: 10 m | Ready in: 25 m

Ingredients
- 2 tablespoons olive oil
- 2 cloves garlic, finely chopped
- 1/8 teaspoon salt
- 1/8 teaspoon ground black pepper
- 1/2 tablespoon crumbled dried red chile pepper
- 1 (28 ounce) can crushed tomatoes
- 1 (6 ounce) can tomato paste

- 1/4 teaspoon celery salt
- 3/4 cup brown sugar, divided

Direction

- In a saucepan, combine olive oil, garlic, salt, pepper and red peppers and lightly sauté over high heat.
- Reduce heat to low and mix in tomatoes and tomato paste. Stir in celery salt, salt and pepper. Start with 1/2 cup of the brown sugar and mix into the sauce. Gradually add brown sugar, depending on acidity of tomatoes. First taste of sauce should be sweet.

Nutrition Information

- Calories: 264 calories
- Total Fat: 7.5 g
- Cholesterol: 0 mg
- Sodium: 768 mg
- Total Carbohydrate: 49.8 g
- Protein: 5.2 g

Canning Pizza Or Spaghetti Sauce From Fresh Tomatoes

"This can be used for either pizza sauce or spaghetti sauce. It can be canned or frozen. Store canned tomato sauce in a cool, dark area."

Serving: 32 | Prep: 30 m | Cook: 1 h | Ready in: 13 h 30 m

Ingredients

- 20 pounds fresh Roma tomatoes

- 1 tablespoon olive oil
- 2 cups chopped onion
- 1/4 cup lemon juice
- 1/4 cup red wine (optional)
- 3 cloves garlic, minced
- 2 tablespoons chopped celery (optional)
- 2 tablespoons minced fresh basil
- 2 tablespoons chopped red sweet pepper
- 2 teaspoons salt (optional)
- 2 bay leaves
- 1/4 teaspoon ground black pepper

Direction

- Fill a large pot with water; bring to a boil. Fill a bowl with ice water. Place tomatoes into the boiling water, working in batches, 30 to 45 seconds. Remove from the boiling water; plunge into ice water. Peel off tomato skins; cut in half. Remove the seeds using your finger or a spoon. Place in a colander to drain.
- Heat olive oil in a skillet over medium heat; place onion into the skillet. Cook and stir until the onions become translucent, about 5 minutes.
- Combine tomatoes, onion, lemon juice, red wine, garlic, celery, basil, red sweet pepper, salt, bay leaves, and ground black pepper in a large pot over medium heat; cook and stir over until tomatoes break down and sauce thickens, about 10 minutes.
- Sterilize 8 pint-size jars and lids in boiling water for at least 5 minutes. Pack tomato sauce into hot,

sterilized jars, filling to within 1/4 inch of the top. Top with clean lids and screw on rings.
- Fill water bath canner with water according to manufacturer's instructions. Bring to a boil and lower jars into the boiling water using a holder. Pour in more boiling water if necessary to bring the water level to at least 1 inch above the tops of the jars. Process for 35 minutes for pints.
- Remove the jars from the water bath canner and place onto a cloth-covered or wood surface, several inches apart, until cool, 8 hours to overnight. Press the top of each lid with a finger, ensuring that the seal is tight (lid does not move up or down at all). Store in a cool, dark area.

Nutrition Information

- Calories: 62 calories
- Total Fat: 1 g
- Cholesterol: 0 mg
- Sodium: 161 mg
- Total Carbohydrate: 12.5 g
- Protein: 2.7 g

Chef Johns Tomato Sauce

"This is one of my most requested food wishes, my all-purpose basic tomato sauce. Whenever I make a meat sauce, this is my base. You can only stir this with a wooden spoon, otherwise it's bad luck."

Serving: 8 | Prep: 15 m | Cook: 1 h 45 m | Ready in: 2 h

Ingredients

- 1/4 cup olive oil
- 1 onion, finely diced
- 1 rib celery, finely diced
- 1 pinch salt
- 4 cloves garlic, minced
- 2 (28 ounce) cans whole peeled San Marzano tomatoes
- 2 teaspoons white sugar
- 1 teaspoon salt
- 1 teaspoon anchovy paste
- 1 teaspoon white wine vinegar
- 1/2 teaspoon dried Italian herbs
- 1 pinch red pepper flakes
- 1 tablespoon tomato paste
- 2 tablespoons chopped Italian flat-leaf parsley
- water, or as needed

Direction

- Place olive oil, onion, celery, and a pinch of salt into a large heavy saucepan or Dutch oven over medium-low heat. Cook until onions are very soft, about 15 minutes, stirring occasionally. Mix garlic into onion mixture and cook just until fragrant, about 1 more minute.
- Pour tomatoes and their juice into a large mixing bowl and use your hands to crush the tomatoes until they look pureed.
- Mix sugar, 1 teaspoon salt, anchovy paste, white wine vinegar, Italian herbs, and red pepper flakes into vegetable mixture. Raise heat to medium and

cook just until liquid has evaporated. Stir in tomato paste and bring to a simmer. Pour in San Marzano tomatoes and parsley. Bring sauce to a simmer, turn heat to low, and simmer for 1 1/2 hours, adding a little water as the sauce cooks down. Stir occasionally.

Nutrition Information

- Calories: 116 calories
- Total Fat: 7.1 g
- Cholesterol: < 1 mg
- Sodium: 674 mg
- Total Carbohydrate: 13 g
- Protein: 2.2 g

Chunky Italian Spaghetti Sauce

"Zesty traditional spaghetti sauce."

Serving: 6 | Prep: 10 m | Cook: 35 m | Ready in: 45 m

Ingredients

- 2 (16 ounce) cans diced tomatoes
- 2 (15 ounce) cans tomato sauce
- 1 tablespoon garlic powder
- 2 teaspoons white sugar
- 2 teaspoons dried parsley
- 1/2 teaspoon salt
- 1/4 teaspoon dried oregano
- 1/4 teaspoon dried basil
- 1/4 teaspoon ground black pepper

Direction
- Combine diced tomatoes, tomato sauce, garlic powder, sugar, parsley, salt, oregano, basil, and pepper in a saucepan; bring to a boil. Lower heat to medium-low, cover saucepan, and simmer until flavors blend, about 30 minutes.

Nutrition Information
- Calories: 76 calories
- Total Fat: 0.3 g
- Cholesterol: 0 mg
- Sodium: 1166 mg
- Total Carbohydrate: 15.1 g
- Protein: 3.4 g

Courtneys Three Tomato Pasta Sauce

"A hearty and simple Italian dish with a zesty touch! This recipe will win over your Valentine!"

Serving: 4 | Prep: 20 m | Cook: 30 m | Ready in: 50 m

Ingredients
- 1/2 pound bulk mild Italian sausage
- 1/2 pound bulk hot Italian sausage
- 1/4 cup olive oil from jar of sun-dried tomatoes
- 1/2 large onion, coarsely chopped
- 3 tablespoons minced garlic
- 1 (28 ounce) can Italian-style diced tomatoes
- 1 1/2 cups oil-packed sun-dried tomatoes, drained and sliced
- salt and pepper to taste

- Italian seasoning to taste
- 1 cup cream
- 1 pound cherry tomatoes, halved

Direction

- Cook mild and hot Italian sausage in a large skillet over medium heat until crumbly and no longer pink. Drain excess grease and set aside. Heat olive oil in the same pan over medium heat; stir in onion and garlic, and cook until the onion has softened and turned translucent.
- Stir in diced and sun-dried tomatoes, and the crumbled sausage; season with salt, pepper, and Italian seasoning to taste. Bring to a boil, then reduce heat to medium-low and simmer for 10 minutes until sun-dried tomatoes have softened.
- Before serving, stir in cream and garnish with cherry tomatoes.

Nutrition Information

- Calories: 756 calories
- Total Fat: 62.5 g
- Cholesterol: 134 mg
- Sodium: 1291 mg
- Total Carbohydrate: 29.4 g
- Protein: 21.9 g

Cucumbertomato Sauce

"This fresh vegetable sauce can be used in place of other sauces, such as traditional spaghetti sauce. It has a sweet fresh taste to it, but is still recognizable as a tomato product. My recommended use is over pasta or with a meat product. In my opinion the sauce is relatively filling and not to be considered a light meal."

Serving: 6 | Prep: 25 m | Cook: 20 m | Ready in: 45 m

Ingredients
- 1/4 cup olive oil
- 2 cloves garlic, minced
- 2 teaspoons dried basil
- 1 cup chopped roma (plum) tomatoes
- 1 teaspoon onion powder
- 1 teaspoon garlic powder
- 1/2 teaspoon red pepper flakes
- 1/2 teaspoon black pepper
- 4 1/2 teaspoons white sugar
- 1/4 teaspoon salt
- 1/2 cup chopped red bell pepper
- 2 cups diced cucumber

Direction
- Heat olive oil in a saucepan over medium heat. Stir in garlic, and cook for a few minutes until fragrant, then stir in the dried basil, and cook for a few seconds more. Add the tomatoes, onion powder, garlic powder, red pepper flakes, black pepper, sugar, and salt. Bring to a simmer, then stir in the red pepper and cucumber. Continue simmering and stirring occasionally until the mixture has reduced to a sauce like consistency, 10 to 15 minutes.

Nutrition Information
- Calories: 115 calories
- Total Fat: 9.2 g
- Cholesterol: 0 mg
- Sodium: 101 mg
- Total Carbohydrate: 8.2 g
- Protein: 1 g

Dads Bolognese Meat Sauce

"This sauce is very different than the other bolognese already listed. It takes a little work, but after you make it once or twice it is really easy... and SO GOOD! My dad used to make it for us almost every weekend, and now I make it for my family!"

Serving: 6 | Prep: 25 m | Cook: 2 h | Ready in: 2 h 25 m

Ingredients
- 1 1/2 pounds ground beef
- 7 carrots, coarsely chopped
- 1 small white onion, chopped
- 4 slices ham
- 1/2 cup butter
- 1 (14 ounce) can beef broth
- 1 (6 ounce) can tomato paste
- 1 lemon, zested
- 2 bay leaves
- 1 pinch dried basil
- 1 1/2 teaspoons ground nutmeg
- 1 tablespoon heavy cream

Direction
- Place ground beef in a large, deep skillet. Cook over medium high heat until evenly brown. Drain, crumble very finely and set aside.
- In a food processor, chop the carrots, onion and ham.
- Melt butter in a large saucepan over low heat. Stir in carrot mixture and simmer for 3 to 5 minutes. Stir

in cooked beef, beef broth, tomato paste, lemon zest, bay leaves, basil and nutmeg. Simmer over lowest heat, partially covered, for at least 2 hours, stirring occasionally.
- Immediately before serving, stir in cream and mix well.

Nutrition Information

- Calories: 469 calories
- Total Fat: 34.3 g
- Cholesterol: 129 mg
- Sodium: 1093 mg
- Total Carbohydrate: 12.8 g
- Protein: 28 g

Delicious Pizza Sauce Recipe

"My child could make this! It's that easy!"

Serving: 4 | Prep: 10 m | Cook: 10 m | Ready in: 20 m

Ingredients
- 2 tablespoons olive oil
- 1 (28 ounce) can crushed tomatoes
- 2 leaves basil, chopped
- 3 cloves garlic, chopped
- 1 pinch salt and ground black pepper to taste
- 1 pinch grated Parmesan cheese

Direction
- Heat olive oil in a saucepan. Pour crushed tomatoes into the saucepan and place over low heat. Stir basil, garlic, salt, and black pepper into the

tomatoes; bring to a simmer. Add Parmesan cheese to sauce to serve.

Nutrition Information

- Calories: 127 calories
- Total Fat: 7.4 g
- Cholesterol: < 1 mg
- Sodium: 263 mg
- Total Carbohydrate: 15 g
- Protein: 3.5 g

Easy Keto Homemade Tomato Sauce

"This easy tomato sauce is perfect for those looking for a quick and low-carb marinara sauce ready to be used with your favorite recipe."

Serving: 6 | Prep: 5 m | Ready in: 5 m

Ingredients
- 1 (28 ounce) can canned San Marzano-style peeled plum tomatoes
- 1/4 cup extra-virgin olive oil
- 1 teaspoon garlic powder
- 1 teaspoon dried basil
- 1 teaspoon salt
- 1/2 teaspoon dried oregano
- 1/2 teaspoon ground black pepper

Direction
- Place tomatoes and olive oil in a blender; pulse until smooth. Add garlic powder, basil, salt, oregano, and pepper; mix until well combined.

Nutrition Information
- Calories: 109 calories
- Total Fat: 9.5 g
- Cholesterol: 0 mg
- Sodium: 575 mg
- Total Carbohydrate: 5.9 g
- Protein: 1.2 g

Easy Meat Sauce

"This is a recipe that you can throw together in 10 minutes and then go and do whatever you want for 1 hour. It is not the thickest sauce, but it is delicious."

Serving: 6 | Prep: 10 m | Cook: 1 h 30 m | Ready in: 1 h 40 m

Ingredients
- 1 tablespoon olive oil
- 1 onion, chopped
- 1 1/4 pounds ground beef
- 2 tablespoons Italian seasoning
- 2 (15 ounce) cans tomato sauce
- 2 (15 ounce) cans fire-roasted diced tomatoes
- 1 teaspoon salt
- 1 splash red wine

Direction
- Heat olive oil in a large skillet over medium-high heat; sauté onion in hot oil until softened, about 5 minutes. Season onion with Italian seasoning; continue to sauté until the herbs are fragrant, about 3 minutes more.
- Break beef into small pieces and add to the skillet; cook and stir until browned and crumbly, 5 to 7 minutes.
- Stir tomato sauce and diced tomatoes into the beef mixture; season with salt, place a lid on the skillet, reduce heat to low, and cook at a simmer for 1 hour.

- Splash wine over the mixture, stir, and simmer until thickened, about 20 minutes.

Nutrition Information

- Calories: 286 calories
- Total Fat: 14.1 g
- Cholesterol: 59 mg
- Sodium: 1553 mg
- Total Carbohydrate: 20.1 g
- Protein: 19.5 g

Easy Pizza Sauce Ii

"My three picky eaters have no complaints about the pizza sauce, and it takes about a minute to make!"

Serving: 16

Ingredients

- 1 (8 ounce) can tomato sauce
- 1/2 teaspoon minced garlic
- 1/2 teaspoon dried oregano
- 1/2 teaspoon dried basil

Direction

- In a medium bowl, combine tomato sauce, garlic, oregano and basil and mix all together. Spread mixture over pizza crust, if desired.

Nutrition Information

- Calories: 4 calories
- Total Fat: 0 g
- Cholesterol: 0 mg
- Sodium: 73 mg

- Total Carbohydrate: 0.8 g
- Protein: 0.2 g

Easy Pizza Sauce Iii

"Quick and easy pizza sauce. No cooking and quick to make."

Serving: 24 | Prep: 5 m | Ready in: 5 m

Ingredients
- 1 (15 ounce) can tomato sauce
- 1 (6 ounce) can tomato paste
- 1 tablespoon ground oregano
- 1 1/2 teaspoons dried minced garlic
- 1 teaspoon ground paprika

Direction
- In a medium bowl, Mix together tomato sauce and tomato paste until smooth. Stir in oregano, garlic and paprika.

Nutrition Information
- Calories: 11 calories
- Total Fat: 0.1 g
- Cholesterol: 0 mg
- Sodium: 148 mg
- Total Carbohydrate: 2.6 g
- Protein: 0.6 g

Essanayes Pizza Sauce

"After trying several brands of store-bought sauce, I decided it was time to make my own. This sauce is great, and super easy to make, but you should refrigerate it overnight to allow the flavors to meld. I started with 1 tablespoon of brown sugar. We all liked the sauce, but I will try it next time with 2 tablespoons of brown sugar. Refrigerate overnight before using. Makes enough for 4 large pizzas."

Serving: 16 | Prep: 5 m | Cook: 45 m | Ready in: 8 h 50 m

Ingredients
- 3 tablespoons olive oil
- 3 cloves garlic, minced
- 1 (28 ounce) can tomato sauce
- 1/2 teaspoon crushed red pepper
- 2 teaspoons dried thyme
- 2 teaspoons Italian seasoning
- 2 teaspoons dried basil
- 2 teaspoons dried oregano
- 1 pinch salt
- 1 tablespoon brown sugar, or more to taste

Direction
- Stir the olive oil, garlic, tomato sauce, red pepper, thyme, Italian seasoning, basil, oregano, salt, and brown sugar together in a saucepan over low heat; simmer, stirring occasionally, for 45 minutes. Refrigerate overnight before using.

Nutrition Information
- Calories: 40 calories
- Total Fat: 2.7 g

- Cholesterol: 0 mg
- Sodium: 257 mg
- Total Carbohydrate: 4.1 g
- Protein: 0.8 g

Everything In The Fridge Pasta Sauce

"Late coming home from work? Kids asking, "What's for dinner?" This chunky sauce is for you. It only takes minutes to make. Serve over angel hair pasta with sprig of fresh basil for garnish."

Serving: 4 | Prep: 10 m | Cook: 20 m | Ready in: 30 m

Ingredients
- 1 tablespoon olive oil
- 4 roma (plum) tomato
- 1 green bell pepper, chopped
- 1 tablespoon chopped fresh cilantro
- 4 cloves garlic, chopped
- 1/4 cup chopped white onion
- 1 (15 ounce) can tomato sauce
- 2 tablespoons grated Parmesan cheese
- 1 (6 ounce) can black olives, drained and sliced

Direction
- Heat olive oil in a large skillet and sauté tomato, green peppers, cilantro, garlic and onion for 5 minutes or so to retain crispness. Add tomato sauce and simmer for 10 to 15 minutes. Mix in olives, parmesan cheese.

Nutrition Information

- Calories: 143 calories
- Total Fat: 9 g
- Cholesterol: 2 mg
- Sodium: 965 mg
- Total Carbohydrate: 14.8 g
- Protein: 3.8 g

Field Grade Spaghetti Sauce

"The delightful surprise ingredient in this sauce is cinnamon, and I guarantee that it's absolutely delicious! In the military, the term "field grade" is for Colonels and Generals, as in "He's a field grade officer." That's how this recipe got it's name...by being the cream of the crop! It's one of the many recipes I've accumulated as a military wife for almost 30 years. This sauce freezes well."

Serving: 8 | Prep: 15 m | Cook: 1 h | Ready in: 1 h 15 m

Ingredients
- 2 pounds lean ground beef
- 2 cloves garlic, minced
- 1/2 cup red wine
- 1 (1 ounce) package dry onion soup mix
- 1 (4.5 ounce) can canned mushrooms, drained
- 2 teaspoons dried basil leaves, crushed
- 1/2 teaspoon salt
- 1/4 teaspoon black pepper
- 1 pinch ground cinnamon
- 1 pinch ground allspice

- 3 tablespoons chopped fresh parsley
- 1 (28 ounce) can crushed tomatoes
- 1 (6 ounce) can tomato paste
- 1 cup water

Direction

- In a large skillet, brown the meat with the garlic over medium heat. Stir in the wine; simmer, stirring often, for 10 minutes.
- Mix in dry onion soup mix, mushrooms, basil, salt and pepper, cinnamon, allspice, parsley, crushed tomatoes, tomato paste, and water. Cover pan almost completely, allowing space for steam to escape, and simmer 1 hour. Add additional water if needed to prevent sticking.

Nutrition Information

- Calories: 377 calories
- Total Fat: 24 g
- Cholesterol: 85 mg
- Sodium: 899 mg
- Total Carbohydrate: 15.2 g
- Protein: 23.3 g

Franks Famous Spaghetti Sauce

"Years of experimenting with many recipes has yielded this recipe that is thick and meaty, yet easy and quick to prepare."

Serving: 8 | Prep: 15 m | Cook: 30 m | Ready in: 45 m

Ingredients

- 1 tablespoon olive oil
- 1 onion, chopped
- 1 green bell pepper, chopped
- 3 cloves garlic, minced
- 4 fresh mushrooms, sliced
- 1 pound ground turkey
- 1 pinch dried basil
- 1 pinch dried oregano
- ground black pepper to taste
- 1 (14.5 ounce) can stewed tomatoes
- 2 (15 ounce) cans tomato sauce
- 1 (6 ounce) can tomato paste

Direction

- In a large skillet over medium heat, sauté onions, green bell pepper and garlic in olive oil until onions are translucent and the peppers are tender. Add the mushrooms, ground turkey, basil, oregano and ground black pepper; fry stirring frequently until the turkey is done.
- Add the can of stewed tomatoes with liquid and reduce heat; simmering until the tomatoes are soft and begin to fall apart. Add the tomato sauce and stir; add tomato paste to thicken. Simmer on very low heat for about 15 minutes. Serve over your favorite pasta.

Nutrition Information

- Calories: 168 calories

- Total Fat: 6.8 g
- Cholesterol: 45 mg
- Sodium: 885 mg
- Total Carbohydrate: 15.6 g
- Protein: 13.3 g

Fresh Sauce With Artichokes And Pine Nuts

"One day, I was at a loss for what to make for dinner. So I scanned my refrigerator and cabinets. This is what developed. It has become a family favorite. Serve over al dente angel hair pasta."

Serving: 8 | Prep: 15 m | Cook: 55 m | Ready in: 1 h 10 m

Ingredients
- 1/4 cup pine nuts
- 2 tablespoons olive oil
- 1 sweet onion, chopped
- 4 cloves garlic, thinly sliced
- 20 roma (plum) tomatoes, chopped
- 2 (15 ounce) cans artichoke hearts - drained, squeezed, and sliced
- 1 tablespoon Italian seasoning
- salt and ground black pepper to taste

- 8 leaves fresh basil
- 1/4 cup grated Parmesan cheese

Direction

- Preheat oven to 350 degrees F (175 degrees C). Spread pine nuts onto a baking sheet.
- Bake in the preheated oven until pine nuts are fragrant and lightly browned, about 8 minutes.
- Heat olive oil in a large skillet over medium heat; cook and stir onion and garlic until onion is softened, 5 to 10 minutes. Add tomatoes, artichoke hearts, Italian seasoning, salt, and pepper; bring to a boil. Reduce heat to low, cover skillet, and simmer until tomatoes have softened, about 40 minutes.
- Stir toasted pine nuts, basil, and Parmesan cheese into sauce; simmer until heated through, about 5 minutes.

Nutrition Information

- Calories: 161 calories
- Total Fat: 6.6 g
- Cholesterol: 2 mg
- Sodium: 693 mg
- Total Carbohydrate: 20.8 g
- Protein: 7.5 g

Fresh Tomato Basil Sauce

"A delicious sauce made with fresh tomatoes and fresh basil. A late summer delight!"

Serving: 6 | Prep: 20 m | Cook: 2 h | Ready in: 2 h 20 m

Ingredients

- 8 pounds tomatoes, seeded and diced
- 1/4 cup chopped fresh basil
- 1 large onion, minced
- 3 cloves garlic, minced
- 1/2 cup olive oil
- salt and pepper to taste

Direction

- In large saucepan, cook tomatoes and basil over medium-low heat until tomatoes are soft.
- Meanwhile, in medium skillet, sauté onion and garlic in olive oil until onions are translucent.
- Add onion mixture to tomato mixture and add salt and pepper. Let simmer on low heat for 2 hours or until thick.

Nutrition Information

- Calories: 330 calories
- Total Fat: 20.6 g
- Cholesterol: 0 mg
- Sodium: 70 mg
- Total Carbohydrate: 37.8 g
- Protein: 6.9 g

Fresh Tomato Sauce

"This is a fresh and delicious pasta sauce that is very simple to make. It is great to make in the summer when there is an abundance of fresh vegetables."

Serving: 6 | Prep: 5 m | Cook: 30 m | Ready in: 35 m

Ingredients

- 1/4 cup olive oil
- 6 tomatoes, chopped
- 3 onions, minced
- 2 green bell peppers, minced
- 4 cloves garlic, minced
- 3 tablespoons white wine
- salt and pepper to taste

Direction

- In a large saucepan, heat oil over medium heat; add tomatoes, onions, green bell peppers, garlic, white wine and salt and pepper to taste.
- Mix ingredients well; cover and simmer for 30 minutes. Serve.

Nutrition Information

- Calories: 144 calories
- Total Fat: 9.4 g
- Cholesterol: 0 mg
- Sodium: 10 mg
- Total Carbohydrate: 13.4 g
- Protein: 2.2 g

Homemade Italian Red Sauce

"You will love my Italian-style sauce. You can add meatballs to this sauce; it comes out really good."

Serving: 12 | Prep: 10 m | Cook: 2 h 10 m | Ready in: 2 h 20 m

Ingredients
- 1/2 cup olive oil
- 1 large onion, minced
- 3 cloves garlic, minced
- 4 cups water
- 2 (32 ounce) cans crushed diced tomatoes
- 1 (16 ounce) can tomato paste
- 1/4 cup chopped fresh basil
- 1 teaspoon baking soda
- 1 teaspoon white sugar
- salt and ground black pepper to taste

Direction

- Heat olive oil in a large saucepan over medium-high heat. Sauté onion and garlic in hot oil until onion is translucent, 5 to 7 minutes.
- Reduce heat to medium-low. Add water, crushed tomatoes, tomato paste, basil, baking soda, and sugar; season with salt and pepper. Stir mixture, bring to a simmer, and cook until the sauce is thickened, about 2 hours.

Nutrition Information

- Calories: 149 calories
- Total Fat: 9.2 g
- Cholesterol: 0 mg
- Sodium: 644 mg
- Total Carbohydrate: 13.9 g
- Protein: 3.1 g

Homemade Italian Sauce

"Sauce like mom used to make. Serve over your favorite pasta. Classic red sauce with onion, mushrooms and garlic."

Serving: 4 | Prep: 20 m | Cook: 1 h 30 m | Ready in: 1 h 50 m

Ingredients

- 1 (16 ounce) can whole tomatoes
- 5 cloves garlic, peeled
- 3 tablespoons olive oil
- 1 white onion, chopped
- 1 pound mushrooms, sliced
- 1 (16 ounce) can crushed tomatoes
- 8 ounces tomato paste
- 1 green bell pepper, chopped
- 2 tablespoons dried oregano
- 1 tablespoon dried basil leaves

Direction

- In a blender chop the whole tomatoes with juice and garlic until chunky. In a medium size pot, heat oil on medium high heat. Put onion and mushroom in and sauté for about 5 minutes.
- Place in pot the blended tomatoes, crushed tomatoes, tomato paste, chopped green peppers, oregano and basil. Bring to boil, then lower to medium low, cover and stir periodically. Cook and reduce about 1 to 2 hours or to your liking.

Nutrition Information
- Calories: 254 calories
- Total Fat: 11.7 g
- Cholesterol: 0 mg
- Sodium: 755 mg
- Total Carbohydrate: 36.4 g
- Protein: 8.7 g

Homemade Pizza Sauce From Scratch

"I noticed that most (all?) the pizza sauce recipes call for either tomato paste or tomato sauce or both. I wanted to do it from scratch! So I experimented until I got it right. This is much better than the store-bought sauce with none of those nasty preservatives."

Serving: 16 | Prep: 10 m | Cook: 1 h | Ready in: 1 h 10 m

Ingredients
- 10 roma tomatoes
- 1 cup water
- 2 tablespoons olive oil
- 1/4 cup white sugar
- 2 tablespoons garlic salt
- 1 tablespoon white vinegar

Direction
- Place tomatoes, water, and olive oil in a blender or food processor; blend until smooth. Transfer tomato mixture to a large pot.

- Stir sugar, garlic salt, and vinegar into tomato mixture and bring to a boil. Reduce heat to medium-low and simmer until thickened, 1 to 2 hours, stirring occasionally.
- Pour tomato sauce into a clean blender or food processor no more than half full. Cover and hold lid down; pulse a few times before leaving on to blend. Puree in batches until tomato sauce is very smooth.

Nutrition Information

- Calories: 35 calories
- Total Fat: 1.8 g
- Cholesterol: 0 mg
- Sodium: 682 mg
- Total Carbohydrate: 4.9 g
- Protein: 0.4 g

Homemade Pizza Sauce Made Lighter

"I say replace sugar with carrots in any tomato recipe. Additional veggies are a sneaky way to get them into the kids. Add olive oil near end of cooking to preserve its flavor."

Serving: 20 | Prep: 15 m | Cook: 30 m | Ready in: 45 m

Ingredients

- 1 green bell pepper, coarsely chopped - or more to taste (optional)
- 1/4 cup coarsely chopped carrot
- 6 cloves garlic, peeled
- 1 (29 ounce) can tomato puree

- 1 (28 ounce) can crushed tomatoes
- 1 tablespoon dried Italian herb seasoning
- 1 teaspoon dried basil
- 1/2 teaspoon red pepper flakes
- 3 tablespoons olive oil

Direction

- Place green bell pepper, carrot, and garlic cloves into a food processor and pulse a few times until the vegetables are very finely chopped.
- Transfer chopped vegetables into a large saucepan. Stir in tomato puree, crushed tomatoes, Italian seasoning, basil, and red pepper flakes; bring to a boil. Reduce heat to low and simmer uncovered until sauce has thickened, about 30 minutes. Stir in olive oil and simmer 1 to 2 more minutes. Sauce may be refrigerated up to 1 week.

Nutrition Information

- Calories: 50 calories
- Total Fat: 2.3 g
- Cholesterol: 0 mg
- Sodium: 215 mg
- Total Carbohydrate: 7.5 g
- Protein: 1.5 g

Homemade Pizza Sauce With Olive Oil

"This is a delicious pizza sauce, quick and easy, and everyone who has it loves it. The olive oil near the end preserves its flavor."

Serving: 8 | Prep: 10 m | Cook: 40 m | Ready in: 50 m

Ingredients

- 1 (28 ounce) can tomato puree
- 1 (28 ounce) can diced tomatoes
- 6 cloves garlic, finely chopped
- 1 tablespoon brown sugar
- 1 tablespoon Italian seasoning
- 1 teaspoon dried basil
- 1/2 teaspoon red pepper flakes
- 3 tablespoons olive oil

Direction

- Bring tomato puree, diced tomatoes, garlic, brown sugar, Italian seasoning, basil, and red pepper flakes to a boil in a large saucepan. Reduce heat to low and simmer uncovered until sauce is thickened, about 30 minutes. Stir olive oil into tomato sauce and simmer until hot, 1 to 2 minutes more.

Nutrition Information

- Calories: 115 calories
- Total Fat: 5.4 g
- Cholesterol: 0 mg
- Sodium: 546 mg
- Total Carbohydrate: 15 g
- Protein: 2.7 g

Homemade Pulled Pork Ragu In An Instant Pot

"Tender pulled pork ragu sauce made easy with an Instant Pot®, with a rich flavor and succulent texture, perfect for your favorite pasta."

Serving: 4 | Prep: 15 m | Cook: 1 h 2 m | Ready in: 1 h 27 m

Ingredients
- 1 1/2 pounds pork tenderloin
- 2 teaspoons salt
- 1/2 teaspoon ground black pepper
- 3 cloves garlic, crushed
- 1 tablespoon olive oil
- 1 (28 ounce) can canned crushed tomatoes
- 1 (7 ounce) jar roasted red peppers, drained and chopped
- 1 tablespoon chopped fresh parsley
- 2 sprigs fresh thyme
- 2 bay leaves

Direction
- Season pork with salt and pepper. Turn on a multi-functional pressure cooker (such as Instant Pot(R)) and select Sauté function. Add garlic and olive oil; cook for 3 minutes. Add pork and cook until browned, about 2 minutes on each side. Add tomatoes, peppers, parsley, thyme leaves, and bay leaves; close and lock the lid. Select high pressure according to manufacturer's instructions; set timer

for 45 minutes. Allow 10 to 15 minutes for pressure to build.
- Release pressure using the natural-release method according to manufacturer's instructions, 10 to 40 minutes. Discard bay leaves, and shred pork with 2 forks.

Nutrition Information

- Calories: 228 calories
- Total Fat: 7.5 g
- Cholesterol: 74 mg
- Sodium: 1680 mg
- Total Carbohydrate: 11.5 g
- Protein: 28.8 g

Homemade Tomato Basil Pasta Sauce

"This amazing sauce is great over noodles or some kind of vegetable. With a short cooking time, it's fabulous!"

Serving: 4 | Prep: 15 m | Cook: 15 m | Ready in: 30 m

Ingredients

- 1 tablespoon butter
- 8 small tomatoes, diced
- 1/4 cup chopped fresh basil
- 1 teaspoon olive oil
- 1 teaspoon garlic salt
- salt and ground black pepper to taste
- 1 tablespoon all-purpose flour
- 1/4 cup water

- 1 clove garlic, grated

Direction

- Melt the butter in a large skillet over medium heat; cook the tomatoes in the melted butter until they begin to fall apart, 5 to 7 minutes. Add the basil, olive oil, garlic salt, salt, and pepper. Slowly stir the flour into the mixture and cook until it begins to thicken, 5 to 7 minutes. Stir the water through the mixture to break up any lumps of the flour. Mix the garlic into the sauce and simmer another 5 minutes. Serve hot.

Nutrition Information

- Calories: 78 calories
- Total Fat: 4.5 g
- Cholesterol: 8 mg
- Sodium: 483 mg
- Total Carbohydrate: 9.1 g
- Protein: 2 g

Homemade Tomato Sauce Ii

"Try the real thing. Delicious tomato, onion and garlic sauce with herbs."

Serving: 6 | Prep: 20 m | Cook: 2 h | Ready in: 2 h 20 m

Ingredients

- 4 tablespoons vegetable oil
- 1 large onion, chopped
- 1 (28 ounce) can crushed tomatoes

- 2 cups water
- 1 (6 ounce) can tomato paste
- 3 leaves fresh basil leaves
- 2 cloves garlic, crushed
- 1 teaspoon salt
- 1 teaspoon ground black pepper

Direction

- In a large saucepan over medium-high heat, sauté onions in the oil until golden brown. Add crushed tomatoes, water, tomato paste, basil, garlic, salt and pepper. Let the sauce come to a boil, lower heat to low and stir occasionally until desired thickness. Sauce is ready when oil rises to the top. Skim off oil.

Nutrition Information

- Calories: 158 calories
- Total Fat: 9.6 g
- Cholesterol: 0 mg
- Sodium: 844 mg
- Total Carbohydrate: 17.8 g
- Protein: 3.8 g

Instant Pot Tomato And Beef Sauce

"Tomato and beef sauce with a hint of wine for your pasta. I've made this fairly basic but feel free to adjust the seasoning to your tastes."

Serving: 6 | Prep: 10 m | Cook: 40 m | Ready in: 1 h

Ingredients

- 1 pound lean ground beef
- 1 teaspoon salt
- 1/2 teaspoon freshly ground black pepper
- 1 large onion, finely diced
- 4 cloves garlic, minced
- 2 teaspoons Italian seasoning
- 1/4 cup dry red wine
- 1 (24 ounce) container crushed tomatoes
- 1 (28 ounce) can whole peeled San Marzano tomatoes, crushed with a fork
- 2 teaspoons lemon juice

Direction

- Turn on a multi-functional pressure cooker (such as Instant Pot(R)). Select Sauté function and adjust the setting to low. Add ground beef and season with salt and pepper. Cook until browned and crumbly, about 5 minutes. Drain and set aside. Add onion, garlic, and Italian seasoning to the pot and sauté until tender, about 5 minutes. Turn Sauté function off.
- Select Sauté function again and adjust the setting to high heat. Sauté for an additional 4 to 5 minutes, stirring infrequently to allow brown bits to form on the bottom of the pot. Pour in red wine to deglaze. Add both tomatoes and browned beef mixture; stir to combine.
- Close and lock the lid. Select high pressure according to manufacturer's instructions; set timer

for 10 minutes. Allow 10 to 15 minutes for pressure to build.
- Release pressure using the natural-release method according to manufacturer's instructions, about 5 minutes. Release any additional pressure carefully using the quick-release method, about 5 minutes. Unlock and remove the lid. Add lemon juice and simmer for 3 to 4 minutes.

Nutrition Information

- Calories: 234 calories
- Total Fat: 11 g
- Cholesterol: 44 mg
- Sodium: 758 mg
- Total Carbohydrate: 17.3 g
- Protein: 16.9 g

Italian Pasta Sauce

"I picked up this recipe when I lived in Italy; everyone loves it. Thought it was time to share! The Merlot and chicken granules are very important ingredients that set this recipes aside from other sauces."

Serving: 18 | Prep: 10 m | Cook: 1 h 5 m | Ready in: 1 h 15 m

Ingredients
- 1 tablespoon olive oil
- 1 large onion, chopped
- 3 large cloves garlic, minced
- 2 (28 ounce) cans tomato sauce

- 1 (28 ounce) can diced tomatoes
- 3/4 cup Merlot wine
- 1 (6 ounce) can tomato paste
- 3 tablespoons chicken bouillon granules
- 3 tablespoons dried basil leaves
- 3 tablespoons Italian seasoning
- salt and ground black pepper to taste

Direction

- Heat olive oil in a large saucepan over medium heat. Cook and stir onion and garlic in hot oil until the onion is translucent, 5 to 7 minutes.
- Sit tomato sauce, diced tomatoes, wine, tomato paste, chicken bouillon granules, basil, Italian seasoning, salt, and pepper with the onion mixture. Bring the mixture to a boil, reduce heat to low, and cook at a simmer, stirring frequently, for 1 hour.

Nutrition Information

- Calories: 64 calories
- Total Fat: 1.2 g
- Cholesterol: < 1 mg
- Sodium: 788 mg
- Total Carbohydrate: 10.1 g
- Protein: 2.4 g

Jackies Vodka Sauce

"This version of vodka sauce has been passed down through a lot of generations. Everyone adds their own special twist. So, if you like, try adding your own."

Serving: 12 | Prep: 10 m | Cook: 1 h | Ready in: 1 h 10 m

Ingredients
- 1 tablespoon olive oil
- 1 onion, minced
- 2 cloves garlic, minced
- 1/2 (6 ounce) can tomato paste
- 1 cup good quality vodka
- 2 (15 ounce) cans crushed tomatoes
- 1 (14.25 ounce) can tomato puree
- 1 teaspoon dried oregano
- 1 teaspoon ground black pepper
- 1 teaspoon salt
- 1 teaspoon dried thyme leaves
- 1 teaspoon dried parsley
- 1/2 teaspoon dried, ground rosemary
- 1/4 cup water (optional)
- 1 cup heavy cream, or as needed

Direction
- Heat the olive oil in a large saucepan over medium heat. Stir in the onion and garlic; cook and stir until the onion has softened and turned translucent,

about 5 minutes. Stir the tomato paste into the onion mixture, working all of the lumps out. Pour in the vodka and bring to a boil over medium-high heat; boil for 1 minute. Add the crushed tomatoes and tomato puree. Season with oregano, pepper, salt, thyme, parsley, and rosemary.
- Return to a simmer; reduce heat to medium-low, cover, and simmer 45 minutes, stirring occasionally. Add water if the sauce becomes too thick as it cooks, but remember that you'll be adding the cream soon, so don't think it too much. Once the sauce has cooked, stir in the cream until the consistency and color are to your liking. Cook another 5 to 10 minutes to reheat.

Nutrition Information

- Calories: 175 calories
- Total Fat: 8.8 g
- Cholesterol: 27 mg
- Sodium: 487 mg
- Total Carbohydrate: 12.3 g
- Protein: 2.7 g

Marias Tomatobasil Spaghetti Sauce

"Homemade tomato sauce that doesn't take hours to make! This sauce can be different every time or can be your own signature sauce, but the basics are the same! Included are directions for using real tomatoes, but if time doesn't permit canned tomatoes will work nicely as well. Enjoy!"

Serving: 8 | Prep: 15 m | Cook: 25 m | Ready in: 40 m

Ingredients

- 8 pounds Roma (plum) tomatoes, peeled and chopped
- 1/2 cup extra-virgin olive oil
- 1 large onion, minced
- 1/4 cup grated Parmesan cheese
- 4 sprigs fresh basil, or more to taste, chopped
- 3 cloves garlic, minced
- 2 tablespoons red wine
- coarse salt and ground black pepper to taste

Direction

- Puree tomatoes in a food processor until smooth; strain through a fine-mesh sieve into a bowl.
- Heat olive oil in a large, deep pot over medium heat. Stir strained tomatoes, onion, Parmesan cheese, basil, garlic, and red wine together in the pot with the oil; season with salt and pepper. Bring the mixture to a boil, reduce heat to medium-low,

and cook at a simmer until thickened, about 25 minutes.

Nutrition Information

- Calories: 231 calories
- Total Fat: 15.7 g
- Cholesterol: 2 mg
- Sodium: 81 mg
- Total Carbohydrate: 20.2 g
- Protein: 5.3 g

Papa Johns Sauce

"Lots of different red sauce recipes out there; this one is superb. Been in the family for over 50 years. If you call your red sauce gravy, you gotta try this! Never understood why my grandpa does, but he is insistent. This recipe also freezes well, so feel free. To defrost, the sauce must thaw for about 6 to 8 hours and reheat in a pot."

Serving: 12 | Prep: 20 m | Cook: 2 h 5 m | Ready in: 2 h 25 m

Ingredients
- 2 teaspoons olive oil, or as needed
- 1 sweet onion, diced
- 6 cloves garlic, minced
- 6 (28 ounce) cans Italian-style peeled tomatoes (such as Cento® San Marzano)
- 2 tablespoons chopped fresh oregano

- 1 tablespoon salt, or to taste
- 1 tablespoon ground black pepper, or to taste
- 10 leaves fresh basil

Direction

- Pour just enough olive oil into a large pot to coat the bottom; place over medium heat. Cook and stir sweet onion in the pot until it releases some moisture, 1 to 2 minutes. Stir garlic with the onion; cook another 1 minute. Remove pot from heat immediately.
- Process the tomatoes in a large food mill using medium holes; grind directly into the pot. Bring the tomato mixture to a light simmer over medium-low heat; season with oregano, salt, and pepper. Allow the mixture to simmer 1 hour, stirring regularly.
- Stir basil leaves into the sauce. Simmer 1 hour more, again stirring regularly.

Nutrition Information

- Calories: 81 calories
- Total Fat: 0.9 g
- Cholesterol: 0 mg
- Sodium: 1295 mg
- Total Carbohydrate: 15.1 g
- Protein: 3.6 g

Pepe Vandels Spaghetti Sauce

"This recipe was brought back from Italy by my husband's grandfather. It is a family favorite! For sauce with meatballs, shape 6 pounds ground beef into balls. After sauce has simmered, place meatballs in sauce and simmer for additional 4 to 5 hours. Stir occasionally."

Serving: 96 | Prep: 30 m | Cook: 4 h | Ready in: 4 h 30 m

Ingredients
- 4 pounds onions
- 6 green bell peppers
- 1 1/2 cloves garlic
- 2 (28 ounce) cans whole peeled tomatoes
- 2 (28 ounce) cans peeled and diced tomatoes
- 1 (28 ounce) can tomato puree
- 2 (16 ounce) cans tomato paste
- 2 (8 ounce) cans tomato sauce
- 1/2 cup vegetable oil
- 2 tablespoons Italian seasoning

Direction

- Grind onion, pepper and garlic in meat grinder. In a large saucepan combine ground vegetables, whole tomatoes, diced tomatoes, tomato puree, tomato paste, tomato sauce, vegetable oil and Italian seasoning. Bring to boil; reduce heat to simmer for 4 to 5 hours. Stir occasionally.

Nutrition Information
- Calories: 39 calories
- Total Fat: 1.3 g

- Cholesterol: 0 mg
- Sodium: 181 mg
- Total Carbohydrate: 6.5 g
- Protein: 1.2 g

Pizza Sauce I

"The Italian flavors of tomatoes, herbs like garlic, basil and oregano are blended with a little cinnamon, sugar, olive oil and parsley to make a fresh saucy pizza base."

Serving: 8 | Prep: 5 m | Cook: 5 m | Ready in: 10 m

Ingredients

- 2 ripe tomatoes
- 1 clove garlic
- 1 tablespoon chopped fresh basil
- 1 pinch ground cinnamon
- 1 teaspoon salt
- 1 pinch ground black pepper
- 1/4 teaspoon white sugar
- 1 teaspoon dried oregano
- 2 tablespoons olive oil
- 1 teaspoon chopped fresh parsley

Direction

- In a food processor, combine the tomatoes, garlic, basil, cinnamon, salt, pepper, sugar, oregano, oil and parsley. Blend without liquifying - should remain a little chunky.

Nutrition Information

- Calories: 38 calories
- Total Fat: 3.5 g
- Cholesterol: 0 mg
- Sodium: 293 mg
- Total Carbohydrate: 1.8 g
- Protein: 0.3 g

Pizza Sauce Ii

"A wonderful, large amount of pizza sauce for any kind of pizza."

Serving: 32 | Prep: 5 m | Cook: 5 m | Ready in: 10 m

Ingredients
- 1/4 cup olive oil
- 1 cup minced onion
- 1/4 teaspoon onion powder
- 2 cloves garlic, minced
- 2 tablespoons dried oregano
- 2 (6 ounce) cans tomato paste
- 2 (15 ounce) cans tomato sauce

Direction
- Heat oil in a medium saucepan over medium heat. Sauté onion, onion powder, garlic and oregano until clear. Stir in tomato paste and tomato sauce; reduce heat to low and simmer for 15 minutes. Let cool and spread over prepared pizza crust.

Nutrition Information
- Calories: 33 calories
- Total Fat: 1.8 g

- Cholesterol: 0 mg
- Sodium: 222 mg
- Total Carbohydrate: 4.1 g
- Protein: 0.9 g

Primo Spaghetti Sauce

"Ok guys, I gotta tell ya I'll eat about anything my wife puts in front of me, but my wife's spaghetti is totally awesome!!! It's pretty spicy, so you may want to cut back on the red pepper and use regular Italian sausage."

Serving: 8 | Prep: 25 m | Cook: 1 h 15 m | Ready in: 1 h 40 m

Ingredients
- 1 pound spicy Italian sausage
- 1/4 cup white wine
- 1/2 onion, chopped
- 1/2 cup sliced mushrooms
- 1/2 green bell pepper, chopped
- 1/4 cup red wine
- 1/4 cup Italian seasoning
- 1 teaspoon crushed red pepper
- 6 bay leaves
- 1 teaspoon dried oregano
- 1 teaspoon onion powder
- 1 teaspoon garlic powder
- 1 teaspoon dried basil
- 1 pinch dried rosemary

- 1 teaspoon ground allspice
- 1 teaspoon salt
- 1/2 teaspoon dried thyme
- 1/2 teaspoon dried sage
- 1/2 teaspoon dried marjoram
- 6 (8 ounce) cans tomato sauce
- 2 (6 ounce) cans tomato paste
- 1/4 cup brown sugar
- 1/4 cup confectioners' sugar

Direction

- Place sausage in a large, deep skillet. Cook over medium high heat until evenly brown. Drain, crumble and set aside.
- In a large pot combine white wine, onion, mushrooms and bell pepper. Cook on medium heat until vegetables are tender. Stir in red wine, Italian seasoning, crushed red pepper, bay leaves, oregano, onion powder, garlic powder, basil, rosemary, allspice, salt, thyme, sage, marjoram, tomato sauce, tomato paste and sausage. Reduce heat, cover and simmer for 45 minutes.
- Stir in brown sugar and confectioners' sugar; simmer, uncovered, for 30 minutes.

Nutrition Information

- Calories: 335 calories
- Total Fat: 18.7 g
- Cholesterol: 43 mg
- Sodium: 1925 mg
- Total Carbohydrate: 30.2 g

- Protein: 12.9 g

Puttanesca Or Kalamata Kwik Sauce

"This is a great quick pasta sauce, full of flavor. Ladle onto short pasta with a generous spoonful of Pecorino Romano cheese. This is not intended to be a sauce that you smother the pasta in. If the fresh tomatoes aren't garden fresh and full of flavor I would consider omitting them from the recipe."

Serving: 4 | Prep: 10 m | Cook: 10 m | Ready in: 20 m

Ingredients
- 1/4 cup olive oil
- 5 cloves garlic, chopped
- 1/4 onion, chopped
- 1 teaspoon crushed red pepper
- 6 sun-dried tomatoes, softened and chopped
- 1 tablespoon capers
- 1 pinch dried oregano
- 2 ripe tomatoes, diced
- 12 kalamata olives, pitted and quartered

Direction
- In a small saucepan, sauté garlic, onions and red pepper. Stir in sun dried tomatoes, capers and oregano. Add fresh ripe tomatoes and kalamata olives. Cook covered for about 5 minutes.

Nutrition Information
- Calories: 182 calories
- Total Fat: 16.8 g

- Cholesterol: 0 mg
- Sodium: 463 mg
- Total Carbohydrate: 7.8 g
- Protein: 1.7 g

Quick Enchilada Sauce

"This recipe is ready to use in about 10 minutes and so much better then the canned sauce in the Mexican foods aisle at your local grocery store. This is a quick, easy version if you don't have the patience or time to completely make from scratch. Hope you enjoy!"

Serving: 12 | Prep: 5 m | Cook: 10 m | Ready in: 15 m

Ingredients
- 1 (15 ounce) can tomato sauce
- 1 (6 ounce) can tomato paste
- 1 1/2 cups beef broth
- 1/2 teaspoon salt (optional)
- 1/4 teaspoon dried oregano
- 1/4 teaspoon ground cumin
- 1/4 teaspoon garlic powder
- 1/4 teaspoon onion powder
- 2 teaspoons chili powder, or more to taste

Direction
- Mix tomato sauce, tomato paste, beef broth, salt, oregano, cumin, garlic powder, onion powder, and chili powder together in a saucepan until smooth.
- Bring sauce to a boil, reduce heat to low, and simmer for 10 minutes.

Nutrition Information
- Calories: 24 calories
- Total Fat: 0.3 g
- Cholesterol: 0 mg
- Sodium: 495 mg
- Total Carbohydrate: 4.9 g
- Protein: 1.5 g

Quick Spaghetti Sauce

"Quick and awesome spaghetti sauce with bell pepper, garlic and onion."

Serving: 6 | Prep: 20 m | Cook: 20 m | Ready in: 40 m

Ingredients
- 1 green bell pepper, chopped
- 1 onion, chopped
- 2 cloves garlic, minced
- 1 (28 ounce) can whole tomatoes
- 2 tablespoons Italian seasoning
- 1 cup chicken broth
- 1 (6 ounce) can tomato paste

Direction
- In a hot skillet, sauté bell pepper and onion on medium-high for 5 minutes. Add garlic and sauté one more minute. Stir in tomatoes and chicken broth. Remove from heat.
- Place mixture in blender and blend until the desired level of chunkiness is achieved. Return to medium-low heat. Stir in tomato paste one tablespoon at a

time until desired level of thickness is reached. Cook for 20 minutes, stirring occasionally.

Nutrition Information

- Calories: 68 calories
- Total Fat: 0.6 g
- Cholesterol: < 1 mg
- Sodium: 572 mg
- Total Carbohydrate: 15.2 g
- Protein: 3.1 g

Roasted Garlic Bell Pepper And Tomato Blender Sauce

"This was a recipe that I created one summer afternoon when I had a big crop of tomatoes from my garden. It is wonderful on pasta with a sprinkle of Romano cheese."

Serving: 4 | Prep: 15 m | Cook: 45 m | Ready in: 1 h

Ingredients
- 5 cloves garlic, chopped
- 1/4 cup water
- 5 tablespoons olive oil, divided
- 6 small tomatoes
- 1 (16 ounce) jar roasted red bell peppers
- salt and pepper to taste
- 1 teaspoon dried red pepper flakes
- 1 tablespoon chopped fresh basil

Direction
- Preheat oven to 450 degrees F (230 degrees C).
- Place whole unpeeled head of garlic in an oven-safe dish with 1/4 cup water and drizzle 1 tablespoon olive oil on garlic. Roast in preheated oven for about 45 minutes.
- Meanwhile, put tomatoes in a blender and blend until pureed. Add bell peppers and blend until pureed.

- Break roasted cloves of garlic and squeeze 5 cloves into blender; blend in garlic. Add 4 tablespoons olive oil and blend briefly. Add salt and pepper to taste, dried red pepper flakes and basil; blend.
- The sauce is ready, but can either be refrigerated for a couple of days to blend the flavors or can be frozen. Sauce can be served cold or heated up until just warm.

Nutrition Information

- Calories: 217 calories
- Total Fat: 17.9 g
- Cholesterol: 0 mg
- Sodium: 416 mg
- Total Carbohydrate: 12.8 g
- Protein: 3 g

Ronnettas Spaghetti Sauce

"This recipe is one my mom used to make and everyone always loved it! It is quick and simple and very delicious! I've found it easy to mash the beef with a potato masher."

Serving: 6 | Prep: 10 m | Cook: 40 m | Ready in: 50 m

Ingredients

- 1 pound lean ground beef
- 2 cloves garlic, crushed
- 1/2 cup grated onion
- 1 packet dry spaghetti sauce mix
- 1 (15 ounce) can tomato sauce
- 1 (6 ounce) can tomato paste
- salt and pepper to taste

Direction

- Cook the beef, garlic, and onion in a large pot over medium-high heat until the beef has browned; stirring often to break up the meat. Stir in the sauce mix, tomato sauce, and tomato paste. Reduce heat to low, and simmer for about 30 minutes, adding water to thin if needed. Season to taste with salt and pepper.

Nutrition Information

- Calories: 213 calories
- Total Fat: 9.6 g
- Cholesterol: 53 mg
- Sodium: 1326 mg
- Total Carbohydrate: 15.2 g

- Protein: 17.5 g

Secret Spaghetti Sauce

"This spaghetti sauce is 'secret' because it has loads of onions and carrots 'hidden' in it. My husband and kids love it - I quadruple the recipe every time and freeze the extra in zip-lock bags."

Serving: 20 | Prep: 20 m | Cook: 40 m | Ready in: 1 h

Ingredients
- 1/2 pound ground beef
- 1/2 pound Italian sausage
- 4 carrots, quartered
- 1 large onion, quartered
- 1 tablespoon olive oil
- 3 cloves garlic, minced
- 1 (30 ounce) can crushed tomatoes
- 1 (30 ounce) can tomato sauce
- 2 tablespoons dried oregano
- 2 tablespoons brown sugar
- 1 tablespoon dried basil
- 1 teaspoon ground black pepper
- 1 teaspoon ground cinnamon
- salt to taste

Direction
- Heat a large skillet over medium-high heat. Cook and stir beef and Italian sausage in the hot skillet until browned and crumbly, 5 to 10 minutes; drain and discard grease.
- Chop carrots and onion in the food processor.

- Heat olive oil in a large saucepan over medium heat; cook and stir carrots, onion, and garlic in the hot oil until onion is transparent, about 5 minutes. Stir ground beef-sausage mixture, crushed tomatoes, tomato sauce, oregano, brown sugar, basil, black pepper, and cinnamon into onion mixture; simmer, stirring occasionally, until flavors have blended, about 30 minutes. Season with salt.

Nutrition Information

- Calories: 95 calories
- Total Fat: 4.7 g
- Cholesterol: 11 mg
- Sodium: 386 mg
- Total Carbohydrate: 9.5 g
- Protein: 4.9 g

Simple Delicious Pasta Sauce

"This sauce is an easy and delicious alternative over what you buy in jars. I use lots of extra garlic in mine! Every time I cook stuffed pastas like asparagus ravioli, my guys asks for this sauce! Don't forget garlic bread and wine!"

Serving: 2 | Prep: 10 m | Ready in: 10 m

Ingredients
- 1 (14.4 ounce) can diced Italian tomatoes
- 4 cloves garlic, minced
- 1/4 cup extra virgin olive oil
- salt and pepper to taste

Direction
- Drain the canned tomatoes. Stir together the drained tomatoes, garlic, and olive oil in a bowl. Season with salt and pepper.

Nutrition Information

- Calories: 296 calories
- Total Fat: 28.3 g
- Cholesterol: 0 mg
- Sodium: 293 mg
- Total Carbohydrate: 10.2 g
- Protein: 2 g

Slow Cooker Italian Spaghetti Sauce

"Thick and rich tomato sauce. I like to cook pork from raw in this recipe."

Serving: 10 | Prep: 5 m | Cook: 4 h | Ready in: 4 h 5 m

Ingredients
- 1 (46 fluid ounce) can tomato juice
- 2 (29 ounce) cans tomato sauce
- 1 (6 ounce) can tomato paste
- 2 tablespoons white sugar, or more to taste
- 1 tablespoon dried basil
- 1/4 teaspoon ground black pepper

Direction
- Stir tomato juice, tomato sauce, tomato paste, sugar, basil, and pepper together in a slow cooker.
- Cook on Low 4 to 6 hours.

Nutrition Information
- Calories: 85 calories
- Total Fat: 0.4 g
- Cholesterol: 0 mg
- Sodium: 1332 mg
- Total Carbohydrate: 20.1 g
- Protein: 3.9 g

Slow Cooker Sauce With Meatballs

"Meatballs with mozzarella tucked inside are slow cooked in a savory tomato sauce and served over pasta for a hearty family meal."

Serving: 6 | Prep: 30 m | Cook: 6 h | Ready in: 6 h 30 m

Ingredients
- Sauce:
- 2 tablespoons extra virgin olive oil
- 1 large onion, chopped
- 6 garlic cloves, minced
- 1 (28 ounce) can RED GOLD® Crushed Tomatoes
- 1 (28 ounce) can RED GOLD® Tomato Sauce
- 1 (6 ounce) can RED GOLD® Tomato Paste
- 1 tablespoon dried basil
- 1 teaspoon dried oregano
- Salt and black pepper to taste
- 1 teaspoon fennel seed
- 2 tablespoons sugar
- 1/2 cup water
- Mozzarella Meatballs:
- 2 pounds lean ground beef or ground turkey
- 1/2 cup quick cooking oats
- 1 teaspoon dried basil
- 1/4 teaspoon black pepper
- 2 cloves garlic, minced
- 2 eggs
- 8 ounces small fresh mozzarella balls

- 3 tablespoons extra-virgin olive oil

Direction

- In a large skillet heat extra-virgin olive oil on medium heat. Add onion and garlic. Cook until tender. Spray 5 quart or larger slow cooker. Add onion and garlic and remaining sauce ingredients. Stir to combine. Cook on low for 6 to 7 hours. Serve on pasta of your choice.
- Meat can be added to the sauce if desired. Below is a meatball recipe that could be added to the sauce at the beginning of the cook time.
- Mozzarella Meatballs: In a large bowl mix turkey, oats, basil, black pepper, garlic cloves and eggs. Shape into 2-inch balls (should get 14 to 16 meatballs). Press 1 small mozzarella ball into center of each meatball, sealed inside.
- In a large skillet, heat oil over medium-high neat. Add meatballs; cook just until browned on all side. Place half of the sauce in slow cooker, add meatballs and then last half of sauce. Cook as directed.

Nutrition Information

- Calories: 709 calories
- Total Fat: 39.9 g
- Cholesterol: 197 mg
- Sodium: 1187 mg
- Total Carbohydrate: 42.5 g
- Protein: 43.7 g

Southernstyle Meat Sauce

"This is my Mom's spaghetti recipe that has been my favorite since the age of three! Great for dinner parties! Serve over spaghetti and with a salad and garlic bread."

Serving: 9 | Prep: 40 m | Cook: 2 h | Ready in: 2 h 40 m

Ingredients

- 3 tablespoons olive oil
- 1 onion, chopped
- 4 cloves garlic, chopped
- 2 pounds ground beef
- 2 (6 ounce) cans tomato paste
- 2 (15 ounce) cans tomato sauce
- 4 tablespoons dried oregano
- 4 tablespoons dried basil leaves
- 3 teaspoons Worcestershire sauce
- 2 tablespoons sugar
- 2 tablespoons red pepper flakes
- 2 (4.5 ounce) cans mushrooms, drained
- 2 bay leaves
- 2 tablespoons salt

Direction

- In a large pot heat olive oil. Add onions and simmer on medium heat until semi soft; stir in garlic. Be careful not to burn. Add ground beef and cook until all pink is gone; drain.

- In pot with drained beef, gently stir in tomato paste and tomato sauce. Mix in oregano, basil, Worcestershire sauce, sugar, red pepper flakes, mushrooms, bay leaves and salt; bring to a boil. Turn heat down to low and simmer for about 2 hours.

Nutrition Information

- Calories: 336 calories
- Total Fat: 19.4 g
- Cholesterol: 61 mg
- Sodium: 2562 mg
- Total Carbohydrate: 21.4 g
- Protein: 22 g

Spaghetti Sauce From The Slow Cooker

"If you want to try something different with your spaghetti."

Serving: 6 | Prep: 10 m | Cook: 6 h 5 m | Ready in: 6 h 15 m

Ingredients
- 1 1/2 pounds ground beef
- 1 (14.5 ounce) can diced tomatoes
- 1/2 cup chopped onion
- 1 (6 ounce) can tomato paste
- 1 tablespoon white sugar
- 1 tablespoon Parmesan cheese
- 1 clove garlic, minced
- 1 teaspoon salt
- 1 teaspoon oregano
- 1/2 teaspoon anise seed
- 1 bay leaf

Direction
- Heat a large skillet over medium-high heat. Cook and stir beef in the hot skillet until browned and crumbly, 5 to 7 minutes; drain and discard grease.
- Stir beef, diced tomatoes, onion, tomato paste, sugar, Parmesan cheese, garlic, salt, oregano, anise seed, and bay leaf together in a slow cooker.
- Cook on Low for 6 to 8 hours.

Nutrition Information
- Calories: 262 calories

- Total Fat: 14.1 g
- Cholesterol: 72 mg
- Sodium: 797 mg
- Total Carbohydrate: 11.4 g
- Protein: 21.5 g

Spaghetti Sauce Iv

"This was my grandmothers recipe. It's easy and very good and I hope you enjoy it."

Serving: 8 | Prep: 20 m | Cook: 2 h | Ready in: 2 h 20 m

Ingredients
- 1/4 cup olive oil
- 6 cloves garlic, chopped
- 3 (28 ounce) cans crushed tomatoes
- 1 pinch salt and pepper to taste
- 1 tablespoon dried parsley
- 8 leaves fresh basil leaves
- 1 cup water

Direction
- In a skillet, heat oil over medium heat; brown garlic lightly. Stir in tomatoes, salt, pepper, parsley and basil. Pour in water and let it come to a boil. Reduce heat to low and cook 2 hours stirring occasionally so it doesn't stick to bottom of pan.

Nutrition Information
- Calories: 158 calories
- Total Fat: 7.6 g
- Cholesterol: 0 mg
- Sodium: 389 mg
- Total Carbohydrate: 22.3 g
- Protein: 5 g

Spicy Creamy Tomato Sauce

"A spicy, creamy tomato sauce with chili, basil, and mascarpone cheese."

Serving: 4 | Prep: 25 m | Cook: 25 m | Ready in: 50 m

Ingredients
- 2 tablespoons olive oil
- 1 large red onion, chopped
- 1 clove garlic, crushed
- 2 (14 ounce) cans diced tomatoes
- 1 teaspoon balsamic vinegar
- 1 teaspoon white sugar
- 1 tablespoon chopped fresh basil
- 1 red chile pepper, seeded and minced
- 1/4 teaspoon salt
- 1/4 teaspoon ground black pepper
- 2/3 cup mascarpone cheese

Direction
- Heat olive oil in a skillet over medium heat, and cook and stir the onion until translucent and soft, about 5 minutes. Add the garlic, and cook and stir for 1 more minute. Stir in the tomatoes, balsamic vinegar, and sugar, and cook over medium heat for 10 minutes, stirring occasionally. Stir in the basil, red chile pepper, salt, and black pepper, and cook

for 10 minutes more. Remove from heat, and stir in the mascarpone cheese.

Nutrition Information

- Calories: 287 calories
- Total Fat: 24.2 g
- Cholesterol: 47 mg
- Sodium: 480 mg
- Total Carbohydrate: 12.6 g
- Protein: 5 g

Sugo Rosso Red Sauce

"This fresh, simple pasta sauce is an Italian staple and a mouthwatering delight."

Serving: 2 | Prep: 10 m | Cook: 15 m | Ready in: 25 m

Ingredients
- 2 large tomatoes
- 2 tablespoons olive oil
- 2 cloves garlic, crushed
- 1/2 teaspoon salt
- 4 large basil leaves, chopped

Direction

- Bring a pot of water to a boil. Cook the tomatoes in boiling water until the skin begins to split, about 1 minute. Immediately remove the tomatoes and plunge into ice water for several minutes to stop the cooking process. Remove the tomatoes from the ice water; remove and discard the tomato skins. Cut the tomatoes into chunks. Blend the tomatoes in a food processor until smooth.
- Heat the oil in a saucepan over medium heat; warm the crushed garlic in the oil until fragrant, being careful not to brown, 1 to 2 minutes. Add the blended tomatoes and salt; bring the mixture to a simmer and cook until the sauce thickens, 10 to 15 minutes. Remove the sauce from the heat and stir the basil through the sauce. Allow the sauce to sit for a few minutes to allow the flavor from the basil to blend into the sauce.

Nutrition Information
- Calories: 157 calories
- Total Fat: 13.9 g
- Cholesterol: 0 mg
- Sodium: 591 mg
- Total Carbohydrate: 8.2 g
- Protein: 1.8 g

Tangy Horseradish Tomato Sauce For Meatballs

"I think this is a tangy, tasty, easy go-to sauce when I need it to be quick and dumped into the slow cooker. I used a recipe similar to this but it only had three of the ingredients and I added more items to make it flavorful and to our liking...hope you do too! We think it goes well with our favorite meatball recipe or as a sauce for our favorite meatloaf."

Serving: 6 | Prep: 5 m | Cook: 3 h | Ready in: 3 h 5 m

Ingredients
- 1 (10.75 ounce) can condensed tomato soup (such as Campbell's®)
- 1 (46 ounce) can tomato-vegetable juice cocktail (such as V8®)
- 3 tablespoons Worcestershire sauce, or to taste
- 1/4 cup dried onion flakes
- 2 tablespoons dried parsley
- 2 tablespoons prepared horseradish
- 1 tablespoon extra-hot Dijon mustard
- 2 teaspoons garlic powder, or to taste
- 1/4 teaspoon black pepper
- 3 tablespoons instant tapioca
- 2 cups water

Direction
- Mix together the tomato soup, vegetable juice cocktail, Worcestershire sauce, onion flakes, dried

parsley, horseradish, Dijon mustard, garlic powder, black pepper, tapioca, and water in a slow cooker. Set the cooker on Low, and cook until thickened, 3 to 4 hours.

Nutrition Information

- Calories: 119 calories
- Total Fat: 0.9 g
- Cholesterol: 0 mg
- Sodium: 1027 mg
- Total Carbohydrate: 25.1 g
- Protein: 3.3 g

www.ingramcontent.com/pod-product-compliance
Lightning Source LLC
Chambersburg PA
CBHW071440070526
44578CB00001B/171